international
mountaintrekking

Design and production

VERTEBRATE **GRAPHICS**

info@v-graphics.co.uk

international
mountaintrekking

A PRACTICAL MANUAL FOR TREKKERS & LEADERS
The official handbook of the
International Mountain Leader Scheme

Written by **Plas y Brenin** instructional team

International Mountain Trekking –
A practical manual for Trekkers & Leaders
The official handbook of the International Mountain Leader scheme

Copyright © 2012   Mountain Training UK

Published by Mountain Training UK
www.mountain-training.org

ISBN 978 0 9541511 7 1

Cover photo: Trekking above Zinal, Switzerland by Bob Timms

All photography by authors unless otherwise credited

Designed, typeset and illustrated
by **Vertebrate Graphics**, Sheffield
www.v-graphics.co.uk

MIX
Paper from
responsible sources

FSC
www.fsc.org   **FSC® C010256**

Printed in China

While every attempt has been made to ensure that the instructions in this book
cover the subject safely and in full detail, the authors and publishers cannot accept
any responsibility for any accident, injury, loss or damage sustained while
following any of the techniques described.

Contents

Our other titles are:

Hillwalking – by Steve Long, 2011, ISBN 978-0-95415-110-2
Rock Climbing – by Libby Peter, 2011, ISBN 978-0-95415-116-4
Winter Skills – by Andy Cunningham and Allen Fyffe, 2011, ISBN 978-0-95415-113-3
Navigation in the Mountains – by Carlo Forte, 2012, ISBN 978-0-95415-115-7

This book is published by Mountain Training UK, which is a registered charity. Revenue from the sale of books published by MTUK is used for the continuation of its publishing programme and for charitable purposes associated with training leaders.

Author's acknowledgements

The staff at Plas y Brenin have an unquenchable appetite to seek out their own adventures at home and abroad and the wealth of experience this brings to their work shines through in the pages of this book. The book itself has been quite a trek, beginning four years ago with a simple concept that as the only provider of all four elements of the International Mountain Leader (IML) training scheme we have a unique insight into educating the people who go on to lead groups in every mountainous region of the globe. Along the way we have been able to involve a great many of our own experts, as well as many of the people we regularly collaborate with. We are immensely grateful for all their help in compiling International Mountain Trekking and while lots of work has gone into checking every detail we would welcome any feedback on the book.

Carlo Forte and Martin Chester have done the majority of the compiling and internal editing of the various chapters as well as writing the 'Navigation', 'Weather', 'Snow – a Seasonal Approach' and 'Snowshoeing' sections. Mike Rosser lectures at the centre on the IML courses and works for our partner organisation Outlook Expeditions and has done a great job writing the 'Planning Your Trip' chapter. Helen Barnard wrote the 'Staying Healthy' and 'Dealing with Altitude' sections and has collaborated closely with Dr Dave Hillebrandt to ensure these chapters reflect the current good practice that his Mountain Medicine Diploma group put forward whenever they are at Plas y Brenin. Mike Raine created the source material for the Environmental Issues chapter, Simon Hale wrote the 'Mountain Hazards' section and Louise Turner wrote about 'Dealing with Problems while Travelling'. Keith Ball provided comprehensive editing for the manuscript and Dave Cheetham compiled the photographs taken by the staff listed above or taken from the Plas y Brenin photo library.

We are grateful to John Cousins for his support throughout the project and to his colleagues within Mountain Training, particularly Mal Creasey and Jon Garside. We also worked closely with Glenmore Lodge and are particularly grateful for the editing feedback and photos from Nigel Williams. Several of our staff are members of the British Association of International Mountain Leaders and so the feedback on the manuscript from the President, Issie Inglis and others within the Association was much appreciated.

Our thanks to Bob Timms, Bob Kinnaird, Will Manners, Caroline Hale and Mo Laurie who have all provided excellent additional photos and Simon Norris at Verterbrate Graphics for creating the first class diagrams. Finally our thanks go to Jane Beagley for her work compiling the book in such a helpful and appealing way.

We hope this manual will greatly assist those taking the journey to become international mountain leaders, and also be useful to mountain travellers venturing abroad.

Martin Doyle
Capel Curig, November 2012

Introduction

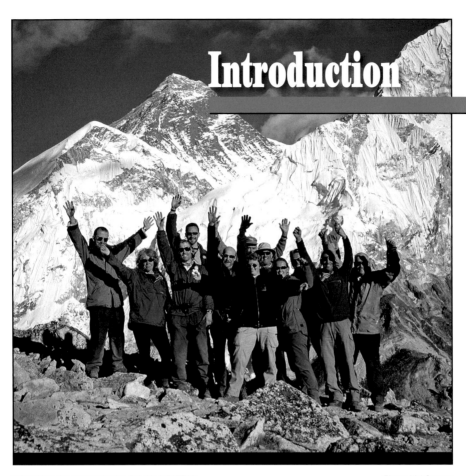

TREKKERS BELOW EVEREST, ON KALA PATTAR

Photo: Mal Creasey

For many people the prospect of exploring somewhere over a period of days, with only unspoilt wild land and a few fellow human beings for company is their idea of the perfect holiday. Walking through the foothills and valleys of the Himalaya, staring across the endless plains of Africa from one of its great summits, traversing the Alps along amazing balcony paths or marvelling at the understory on a jungle trek is all the stuff of dreams.

FIGURE 1.01   TREKKING IN THE TRIGLAV NATIONAL PARK, SLOVENIA   Photo: Helen Barnard

While trekking can be done alone it invariably involves others and for most people this greatly enriches the experience. Whether trekking with best mates or strangers thrown together as part of an organised expedition it would be rare to come back without a few insights into human nature and hopefully a few firmer friends.

A further attraction is the chance to meet and spend time in the company of indigenous people, be they Alpine herdsmen turned hut Guardians or Nepali farmers earning extra cash as porters. Once you have immersed yourself into their mountains these people's knowledge and connection to the land is something most westerners lost long ago.

Seeing sights and meeting people is not enough for the trekker: they need to earn the view, be surprised by nature and perhaps even look forward to an element of adventure. Trekking is about effort and adventure in wild places and for that every individual wants a head start in trying to work out if they are up to the challenge.

1.1 Who is this book for?

This book is for anyone setting out on an overseas walking trip, whether it is the Tour du Mont Blanc or a trek around the Towers of Paine. The content is derived from personal experience and from the training scheme which originated in Europe for the International Mountain Leader (*see Appendix A.3 on page 174*). While this scheme is designed for professionals much of the advice and ideas are applicable to all; the text is for everyone – novice or seasoned explorer.

1.2 Risk and responsibility

British Mountaineering Council Participation Statement
It is worth at this stage remembering that anyone that seeks any level of adventure must recognise that risk is a fundamental part of the experience ('adventure' being a journey with an uncertain

FIGURE 1.02   INDONESIAN VILLAGE CHIEF
Photo: Mal Creasey

FIGURE 1.03   WHICH WAY?   Photo: Mike Rosser

outcome). The British Mountaineering Council has a participation statement as follows: *the BMC recognises that climbing, hill walking and mountaineering are activities with a danger of personal injury or death. Participants in these activities should be aware of and accept these risks and be responsible for their own actions.*

possible to use and adapt the information to suit a variety of different situations.

The material in this book is in no way intended as a substitute for personal experience. We trust that readers will find many practical suggestions to help plan and conduct a safe journey in the hills and mountains around the world. We hope that the fruits of our collective experiences may help readers to avoid revisiting some of our mistakes. Every day spent trekking teaches us all something new both about ourselves and our surroundings. The famous naturalist **John Muir** put this succinctly: 'In every walk with nature one receives far more than he seeks'.

Enjoy your trekking!

1.3 About this book

While this book is mainly concerned with trekking in the mountains of the world the information and principles detailed are transferable to a variety of other trekking environments. Throughout the book the term '**trekker**' is used to represent anyone going for a walk but perhaps with a certain emphasis on long (possibly multi-day) trips with a degree of remoteness to the journey.

This book can be read from cover to cover; however it is designed as a reference text, with comprehensive index and contents allowing the reader to research specific issues. By giving ideas and principles without prescribing specifics it is

1.4 Leadership

The process of adapting leadership skills acquired in the UK to taking sole charge of a group of clients on expedition is one that requires some thought. Living with clients for an extended period of time takes some getting used to as does dealing with issues among those thrown together. Managing everyone's ambitions and expectations requires good communication skills, diplomacy and at times authoritative leadership. Compared to a day trip there are inevitably more complex decisions to be made. Often the group is a large one, creating complex dynamics,

FIGURE 1.04   TREKKING NEAR TOUBKAL, MOROCCO   Photo: Helen Barnard

which may result in real peer and group pressure. Add to this the involvement of local guides and the leader's challenge is set.

Expectations of the client often point the way to defining the qualities required of a leader; however there is more. Leadership is not a science to be learnt from a book or course but an art developed over time. It's not a set of rules to be followed, but an ability to build relationships. And while skills and techniques play a role it is more about a blend of personality and style. Good leaders will have intuition, empathy and common sense to help realise the most appropriate style to take when working with any particular group. They may from time to time tell people what to do; however leadership is not just about giving directions – it's also about empowering people to do what's needed in the best possible way. Good leaders depend on earning trust from those they lead and rather than demanding performance they inspire it. Some people will naturally make better leaders than others, but with time and experience it is possible for everyone to become a competent leader. The ability to reflect and analyse our own performance in an objective manner is one of the keys to developing and succeeding as a good leader.

1.4.1 Clients may expect their leader to:
- be good at planning and organising
- be self confident
- be technically competent
- be experienced and knowledgeable
- be able to demonstrate an appropriate level of care for other people
- be able to make good decisions
- be trustworthy
- be able to communicate well
- be able to build and maintain morale
- be able to inspire others
- be able to deal with difficult situations and possibly conflict
- be able to anticipate problems and deal with them proactively
- be able to build and work with groups
- be able to assess the needs of individuals and manage the trek as needs evolve.

It goes without saying that any company wishing to employ a trek leader would also look for the same qualities; however they often require specific attributes to suit both the nature of their clients and the destinations.

FIGURE 1.05   STOK KANGRI TREK   Photo: Peter Stacey

- Specific experience: knowledge of the country, route and even the type of clients to be looked after and experience of working with agents/guides.
- Qualifications: to satisfy any guidance or regulations.
- Previous leadership experience.
- Specific training e.g. wilderness/remote area first aid.
- Incident management training/experience.
- Language skills: may be required for certain destinations to help communicate and liaise with the local people.
- Environmental awareness: an awareness of the specific environmental issues on any particular trip so as to educate and involve clients in helping reduce impact.
- Knowledge or experience of using communications: radios, sat-phones or emergency position-indicating radio beacons (EPIRBs).

Making serious decisions or resolving problems in remote situations can be stressful for any leader. However it provides comfort for a leader in these situations to know they have the backup and support of their employer even if they are thousands of miles away. Nowadays with modern technology and the invention of sat-phones it is possible to gain support and advice from almost anywhere provided there are good systems in place beforehand. A leader being employed to run a trek on behalf of an organisation would expect more than remuneration in return for services especially when working in distant countries or remote locations. The minimum expected would be as follows:

- On-going support throughout the trip
- Training
- Briefing
- Logistical support
- Insurance
- Contract
- Communications
- Incident and emergency support
- Client information (medical disclosure, age, etc.)
- Wages/salary
- Specific group safety equipment

The many situations and decisions to be faced on an expedition can, of course, never be fully predicted. This uncertainty is part of the fun, but it can also be the source of conflict and danger. It is the management of a diverse range of ever-

FIGURE 1.06   ORGANISING LOGISTICS AT A REMOTE DROP OFF IN GREENLAND   Photo: Nigel Williams

changing factors that makes the leader's role both complex and dynamic. That said, leading groups of people on such expeditions can be extremely rewarding, offering the opportunity to educate, develop and inspire individuals in unique ways, while at the same time achieving all this within ourselves.

Throughout the text reference is made to leadership issues and highlighted in shaded boxes.

Planning your trip

TREKKING IN THE VALAIS, SWITZERLAND

Photo: Bob Kinnaird

Trekking expeditions can be diverse
in nature with many changing and
even conflicting factors contributing
to the adventure.

2

FIGURE 2.01   BEGINNING THE TREK   Photo: Steve Long

A journey over high peaks and passes will require a very different approach to one travelling through lower valleys and plains. It may be self supporting, with participants each carrying their own food and equipment or alternatively it may be supported by porters, guides, cooks and pack animals. An expedition in Europe following well marked trails from one mountain hut to another with good food and sleeping facilities will have a very different feel to one in a remote region with poor maps. The latter will require more detailed planning and research, often with support from agents within the country to help co-ordinate logistics, equipment, transport and food requirements, as well as planning for emergencies. This chapter focuses on the planning and organisation of remote trips, although much of the advice can be used when travelling to more developed countries and on shorter trips.

2.1 The expedition leader

Anyone taking on the role of expedition leader should be prepared to organise multi-day trips and journeys, whether hut-based or using alternative accommodation. This may involve arrangement of transport including flights, equipment, food requirements and accommodation. While it may be possible to plan this in advance some fine-tuning of the detail may have to take place in-country. Knowledge of the local language and customs will help in these situations. This may involve the use of crib cards, phrasebooks or learning some useful phrases. It is important to give sympathetic consideration to cultural differences within the chosen country.

Aside from the qualification of International Mountain Leader (IML) *(see **Appendix A.3** on page 174)* the British Standards Institute have a standard to give guidance to planners and leaders of all types of expedition whether adventurous, research, commercial or amateur (BS8848). This gives a set of criteria by which an individual or group can match its competence as well as providing guidance as to the key areas to address when planning and leading an expedition. These

FIGURE 2.02   HIGH CAMP, NEPAL   Photo: Mal Creasey

include route planning, finance, setting aims and objectives, flights and travel, in-country support and staying fit and healthy. As the great Himalayan explorers Tilman and Shipton said: 'Time spent in research and planning is never wasted'. Leaders organising expeditions may also need to ensure they adhere to the European Package Travel Regulations 1992.

2.2 Gathering information and choosing a route

The first stage in any successful expedition is planning and research. Information on an area or region may come from a variety of sources including friends, magazines, books, websites and organisations such as the Mountaineering Councils (British Mountaineering Council, Mountaineering Council of Scotland, Mountaineering Ireland), Royal Geographical Society (RGS), Geography Outdoors Expedition Advisory Centre and the Young Explorers Trust (YET).

There are a number of commercial companies and individuals offering trekking expeditions who will also do all the research and preparation for the clients, who then only have to turn up and enjoy the planned journey. Searching the internet will give details of these and the destinations they offer.

 Leader's Information

Youth Expeditions
If organising an expedition for a school or youth organisation the Expedition Providers Association (EPA), the representative body for Commercial Providers of Overseas Expeditions for School and Youth Groups, would also be a good resource. Many people will also be accredited through the Council for Learning Outside the Classroom 'Quality Badge' Scheme or BS8848.

2.3 Establishing a goal

Each trekking expedition will have some planned objectives such as exploration, research, adventure, a summit or simply a journey between two places along an interesting route. The participants may have similar or differing interests that motivate them to participate in the same journey. These may include interests in people, culture, adventure, photography, flora, fauna, painting, history, food and wine. This bringing together of people from different backgrounds and with different interests can make or break a trek team. Too many diverse interest groups could prevent the team from gelling and individuals may feel compelled to stop at places that are of little or no interest to them. A group discussion facilitated by a skilful leader can have a positive effect.

2.4 Managing group expectations

When choosing a destination or route with or on behalf of a group it is important to consider the level of challenge the trek will present. Matching this with the group's expectations and ambitions is crucial. If the trek is too easy for the group they will be under-stimulated and bored and if the clients having paid for a 'challenging adventure' they may have real reasons for complaint. Conversely if the trek is too physically demanding it is likely to end in failure or even accident or injury. Many potential problems can be avoided by carefully matching the group to the trek.

 Leader's Information

Inclusive leadership

Looking after clients for a prolonged period of time can provide a range of challenges even for the most experienced leaders. As a trip begins, relationships are formed that then mature throughout the course of the journey. In some cases these relationships may break down for a number of reasons: tiredness, personality clashes or conflict of interests. Either way this can present an awkward situation for a leader to resolve and can have a detrimental effect on the success of the expedition. In these situations a leader needs to have a range of qualities that allows them to listen, communicate and help to resolve issues with the minimum amount of disruption. This is 'easier said than done'. From the outset a leader can reduce the potential for problems to arise by considering a more inclusive approach. One of the keys to a successful expedition is for the leader to understand the needs of the team, task and individuals and try to foster an environment that allows for open discussion and debate. By including everyone in the decision-making process it allows each person to comment and feel they have ownership of the trip. Good delegation of tasks by the leader will create less work for everyone and give more duties to the team enabling them to have more responsibility but in a more practical way. The goal for any leader is to try and produce a 'well oiled machine', with everyone working for a common goal but in a way that benefits each individual. Living together day in, day out can be stressful especially if conditions and situations conspire against you. Everyone needs some down time away from the group or from tasks to recharge their batteries. Recognising this, time should be factored into any itinerary for people to relax and 'kick back' for a while.
It is just as important to factor yourself (the leader) into these plans, making sure where possible there is some time for you. By relaxing and spending short periods of time apart it can rejuvenate relationships and increase morale.
If these breaks are timed carefully to coincide with a new phase of the journey they will often re-energise the trip.

The initial interest may come from reading a book or magazine article, watching a TV programme, talking to friends, reading a brochure or searching on the Internet. Interest may lie in well established treks such as to Everest Base Camp in Nepal or the Cordillera Huayhuash circuit in Peru or you may wish to seek out more remote and unexplored areas. Getting off the beaten track often gives a more satisfying trekking experience as there is less chance of meeting other trekkers and a greater chance of meeting and interacting with local people.

2.5 Permits and travel restrictions

You may need to obtain an entry visa prior to travelling to a destination country, for example to India; increasingly this can be done online. Also check to make sure you are getting the correct visa; even visiting a project may require more than a 'tourist' visa. Many destinations require passport details to be sent to the relevant embassy, in which case be prepared for this process to take several weeks, and maybe consider visiting the embassy in person.

If the party consists of individuals who are nationals of different countries the entry requirements may be different for each. For some destinations there may be a requirement to obtain an entry visa on arrival. Often the airline travelled

with will provide a form to fill in during the flight and there may also be customs forms to complete.

The Foreign and Commonwealth Office (FCO) and embassy websites will provide up-to-date advice on the destination to which you are travelling as well as listing travel restrictions.

It may be beneficial to inform the British Embassy and embassies of other nationals in the party of your dates of travel and itinerary while in-country. They can provide invaluable help in the event of an emergency. This can now be done online for many destinations.

2.6 Insurance

Insurance for any overseas trip is essential. The cost of unforeseen expenses arising from accidents, illness, natural disasters or theft can be considerable. Protecting yourself against a potential finance disaster is paramount. Even if you are travelling no further than Europe it should still be a requirement before departure. This is because, unlike the UK, many countries will charge for rescue and medical facilities and even with a European health card the cost of a rescue operation can reach many thousands of pounds. Insurance can protect the individual from such costs; policies with all manner of products are available to cover every aspect of trekking. Before buying any policy take time to read the small print so that you are fully aware of what is being covered and what is excluded.

FIGURE 2.03   CHECKPOINT ON KILIMANJARO

Photo: Iain Peter

FIGURE 2.04   WINTER RESCUE   Photo: John Cousins

There are other points to consider.

- **Restrictions:** age, altitude, terrain and activities.
- **Baggage:** what is covered and is this a 'new for old' policy.
- **Medical cover:** the recommendation is for £1 million per person in Europe and £2 million worldwide. Check to make sure this also includes emergency dental treatment, travel and accommodation for those travelling with the incapacitated person and repatriation to the UK in the event of a serious injury or fatality.
- **Search and rescue:** this must cover helicopter evacuation, which in some countries may be extremely expensive.
- **Additional activities:** many trips will involve the opportunity to try a different activity, such as mountain biking. Your policy may not provide cover for additional activities, there-fore meaning you could be excluded in this situation. Often a simple call to the company will allow additions to be made. Depending on the activity and level of risk there may be no extra charge.

When travelling to sensitive areas, especially against the advice of foreign embassies or agencies (FCO), it is unlikely that a standard policy will cover the trip. Some companies are prepared to take the risk and insure such expeditions; however the small print will need to be read thoroughly before departure and it is likely the premium will be increased to suit. War and terrorism are potential risks when travelling to certain areas And many policies exclude for both these situations; however some companies do cover with maybe fewer exclusions. Apart from total exclusion for both situations, two other options may be available.

- Full cover for terrorist acts but war is excluded.
- Full cover for terrorist acts and war; war cover only if one of the five major powers is **not** involved.

Make sure you take the relevant insurance documents on the trip and leave copies with a contact at home or scan important documents (passport, insurance, itinerary) and be able to access them via the internet and web mail. If working with an in-country agent leave important details with them in case international communication is not possible. These documents will provide detail of your cover but also the relevant contact details of who to call in the event needing assistance and a claim. Although an insurance company will sell a policy it is unlikely they will co-ordinate any emergencies. Contracted companies with the necessary expertise usually do this. In the case of more remote trips this may be subcontracted further to a local in-country organisation. Either way it can mean any issue takes longer to resolve as communication between a range of different organisations can delay proceedings. If possible try to find

Insurance

Leaders looking after others can also obtain insurance to protect against any claims made against them. This is particularly important when you are legally responsible for members of a group and their actions, as in the case of working with school groups.

However the situation with legal liability cover and overseas expeditions is not straightforward. Outside the UK countries have their own laws that will vary greatly from place to place. As a result an action against an individual may not be issued in the UK. Ensure that any policy purchased has a world-wide jurisdiction and appropriate cover for the countries visited and for clients from other countries.

FIGURE 2.05   ARRIVING AT PUERTO MALDONADO IN THE AMAZON BASIN, PERU   Photo: Outlook Expeditions

- Customs and good practice in the destination country
- Useful words
- Health and hygiene
- Advice for girls and women
- Altitude and acclimatisation
- Expedition fitness

out what the arrangements are in the event of requiring assistance and obtain contact details for the relevant organisations. This may well reduce time when dealing with an emergency.

On a final note talk to the insurance company in an open and honest manner with regards to the nature of the trip. Once armed with all the information they will then offer the most appropriate policy for your needs and set a premium accordingly.

2.7 Information for your group

Producing a dossier of information can help ensure every one is well informed as to the nature of the expedition and the itinerary. This can be e-mailed or even sit on a website. Include the following:

- Dates
- Costs stating inclusions and exclusions
- Flight information
- Insurance
- Itinerary
- Heath and medical advice including vaccinations required
- Advice on visas/permits
- Equipment – personal and group

If you are organising the expedition for a group you will require some information from them.

- Personal contact details
- Next of kin and emergency contact
- Medical history including any medication to be taken during the expedition
- Details of insurance taken out including policy number and contact details
- Photocopy of passport – in case it is lost
- Any dietary requirements
- Spare passport photos can also be invaluable

2.8 Travel to your chosen destination

Part of the adventure may be getting to your chosen country or region by public transport, car or train but most expeditions will begin with a flight. Researching who flies, from where, what their weight allowances are and the cost of freight will normally require some time. There are many travel websites that can help as well as those of individual airlines. A large party, usually 10 or more, may be able to book as a group with some savings. However, in some cases they can be more expensive.

Flights may be booked directly with an airline or through a travel agent. If booking a package through a commercial provider flights may or may not be included. It's important to ensure that any monies paid are safeguarded and that any booking agents have appropriate security such as an Air Traffic Operators Licence (ATOL) and an Association of Bonded Travel Organisers Trust Ltd (ABTOT) Bond, who can both provide financial security.

2.9 Travel within your destination country

Internal flights within destination countries are not covered by ATOL or ABTOT *(see 2.8 Travel to your chosen destination)* unless they are booked prior to leaving the UK and are part of a flight package. These flights are often booked separately either online, through a local in-country agent or by yourselves on arrival.

FIGURE 2.06   TRAVELLING IN BOLIVIA   Photo: Jon Garside

FIGURE 2.07   TREKKING WITH MULES, NORTH OF CUSCO, PERU   Photo: Outlook Expeditions

FIGURE 2.08   BAGGAGE CARRIER   Photo: Outlook Expeditions

Prior booking or knowledge of the flight schedules of these smaller companies may save many days of waiting in small airports. Some flights to mountain airstrips are limited by time of day and weather. These smaller aircraft may have a lower baggage weight allowance compared to international flights so this is worth checking in advance. Often the operating companies will only charge a few pounds per kilo for excess baggage unlike the international carriers who will charge many tens of pounds per kilo.

Most fun and memories will come from journeys made by bus, train, taxi or boat. Public transport can be the most engaging with plenty of opportunities to meet local travellers and their livestock!

If making travel arrangements in-country you'll find that guidebooks such as *Lonely Planet* or *Rough Guides* will help with where to catch buses and trains and give an idea of costs and timetables.

It is usually easy to negotiate private hire vehicles either independently or via a local agent. These may be self-drive cars, 4x4s or a bus. Beware that standards will be different to those of the UK and Europe. Try and find out what sort of vehicle and driver licensing there is and ensure everyone is aware of what to expect.

Before departure satisfy yourself that the transport offered is of an acceptable standard and be prepared to ask for an alternative if you feel that it may compromise safety.

Check the condition of the vehicle, seat belt use, driver health and ability and the condition of the roads. The leader should also have the means and courage to communicate with a poor driver.

Finally avoid travel at night. There have been instances of tourist buses being stopped and passengers robbed plus there is the danger of collision with other motorists not using lights!

2.10 Specialist accommodation – Alpine huts

All the European Alpine Countries have a well managed system of high mountain huts, most with a Guardian resident throughout the late spring/summer months. In the autumn and winter there is unlikely to be any resident staff; however most will have a winter room consisting of a dormitory and somewhere to cook. This is replicated in other mountain areas such as New Zealand. Some huts are private and many are run

FIGURE 2.09 TYPICAL ALPINE HUT, THE RIFUGIO ALIMONTA, THE ITALIAN DOLOMITES Photo: Bob Kinnaird

FIGURE 2.10 DINNER TIME IN A BUSY ALPINE HUT Photo: Bob Kinnaird

through alpine associations who provide discounts for their members.

In high season huts must be pre-booked to ensure a bed and many places limit the size of group they can accommodate. In Corsica for example group bookings for huts on the GR 20 are limited to 10. If planning a multi-day trek it's best to make all the bookings before setting off although it is often possible to book by ringing ahead if your plans are flexible. Many of the huts are small so groups can take a light weight tarp and sleeping bags to sleep under outside the hut. Don't expect 5-star services but most staff will be welcoming and friendly. In some regions such as the Slovakian High Tatras Mountains these may even have a hotel feel about them with beds supplied with linen, but mostly these will be robust stone and wood buildings, with dormitory rooms containing 'alpine bunks' where between 3 and 50 persons can share a memorable sleeping experience! There is no need to bring a sleeping bag as there will be a pillow and 1 or 2 blankets per person. You may need to bring a light weight cotton liner to sleep in and a pillow case.

Huts managed by a Guardian will offer a dinner, bed and breakfast service but those with special dietary needs may need to take food with them or at least inform the Guardian as to any requirements. Some huts will cook the food that you bring and others will have a simple kitchen area for cooking your own meals but be aware that liquid fuels may not be allowed inside the hut. If bringing your own lunch you may have to eat this outside.

Most huts will not allow boots inside and should have racks of slippers and clogs to wear. Sign in as soon as you arrive and confirm your room allocation and meal times. Finally arrange a time for breakfast or confirm the time it is being served. Remember to clear up after meals, keep rooms tidy, fold away blankets and offering to assist with washing up after meals is often welcomed.

FIGURE 2.11 INSIDE A TEA HOUSE IN NEPAL
Photo: Caroline Creasey

Most huts will have cold running water but hot water usually needs to be boiled (showers, if any, are likely to be cold). Some huts will have flush toilets but many will be a long drop – often sited just away from the main building. A head torch is essential for finding your way about after lights out as electricity is generator powered and this will be switched off at night.

Prices may vary depending upon whether you are a member of an Alpine Club or National Mountaineering Association.

Most huts will have a phone and radio. Carrying their numbers with you can assist with booking ahead even if you have not fully planned your route. It is also good etiquette to inform the hut if you are delayed or not planning to stay that night. They will also assist with rescue call outs. The staff will also be a font of knowledge about routes, the weather and the local conditions.

During the middle of the day the huts are often bustling with day visitors getting lunch and drinks. The evenings may be quieter depending on how many persons are staying the night. Most will have a policy of no noise after about 10pm. Remember you could be sharing the hut with mountaineers that are getting up in the early hours.

FIGURE 2.12   A TREKKERS CAMPSITE   Photo: Outlook Expeditions

2.11 Accommodation further afield

When you arrive in-country in more exotic and far away destinations you may well spend a few days in a town or city such as Quito in Ecuador (2850m) or La Paz (3636m) in Bolivia where you will find yourself at altitude. This may also be part of your acclimatisation process. If arriving at night consider pre-booking transport to the accomodation and being met at 'Arrivals'.

Whether you stay in a budget hostel or 5-star hotel it is important to stay fit and healthy. It is also worth considering personal security, the water supply and to check for bare wires, etc. Pre-booking accommodation based on prior know-ledge or recommendation can make for an easier start to your expedition, especially if arriving late at night after a long flight.

Fire regulations may differ from the UK and the EU. Familiarise yourself and your team with any fire exits and have an agreed meeting point. Many hostels will not have fire alarms so if practical carrying one or two battery powered smoke alarms could provide some warning in the event of a fire.

FIGURE 2.13   AN UNSTAFFED HUT   Photo: Nigel Williams

If taking camping equipment from the UK, carry out a thorough check prior to departure. Poor tents that leak or have zips that don't work can make an otherwise perfect journey through the mountains a miserable experience. If hiring equipment in-country try to check the make and quality of the tents before the trek starts. Carrying some zip lube and a tent repair kit will allow most problems to be solved *(Gaffer tape and zip lock bags are the answer to most repairs but also see **Appendix A.2** on page 170).*

FIGURE 2.14   MONSOON TREKKING   Photo: Outlook Expeditions

In some countries such as Nepal and Morocco, tea houses or gites may be used for sleeping en-route. Make sure you and your team know what is being provided; often you will need sleeping bags, toilet rolls, etc. In some of the

more popular high mountain areas of Bolivia and Ecuador trekkers may spend a night in a mountain hut similar to a hut in the Alps; however these are unlikely to be serviced.

Some of your team may prefer single rooms or tents to sharing with others. When trekking at altitudes above 3000m be aware of people sleeping on their own – should they become ill at night they may not be able to attract the attention of others. Never let any one you suspect of suffering with altitude or a serious medical condition sleep alone.

 Leader's Information

Prior knowledge of the area

When leading others having prior knowledge of the route or having previously visited the country or region can be an advantage. Many treks will be supported by an in-country guide and agent who can supply some of this knowledge. Part of the fun and adventure of trekking is visiting areas which you may not have been to before but for a more formally led group your clients may feel more reassured if you know the chosen route and have considered issues of safety, route options and are aware of likely flora, fauna and local customs.

2.12 Seasons

Choosing the best time of year to go and the expected weather can be an important part of your planning. *Chapter 8* gives more detail on how the weather and climate may influence a trip; however it is an important aspect to consider during the planning phase.

FIGURE 2.15 PORTER SELECTION, KARAKORUM
Photo: Iain Peter

2.13 Permits

To trek in some areas you may require permits. These can sometimes be bought at the 'Park Gate' or it may require prior permission such as when trekking in some areas of Ladakh in India. To obtain these permits you may need passport-sized photographs, copies of passports or entry visas so be prepared.

In some areas such as the Kilimanjaro National Park entry visas may be paid for on a day by day basis. In the case of Kilimanjaro this can be more than one hundred dollars per day. This can be a hidden cost to an expedition so it is advisable to research the requirements and to include this in the expedition budget.

2.14 Financing

If your expedition breaks new ground by travelling to remote unexplored areas or by having a research element then it may be possible to apply for grants from organisations such as the Mount Everest Foundation, Winston Churchill Memorial Trust and the mountaineering councils (BMC, MCofS and MI). There are also many local trusts, charities, research bodies and commercial organisations that may support your expedition depending on its objectives or the interests of the group. Treks where part of the purpose is to raise money for a charity are increasingly popular.

Make sure you have a secure method of sending payments overseas. You may use bank transfers or credit/debit cards. If some payments are in cash then you have to decide whether to take a lot of currency with you or use in-country ATMs or banks. Check with any in-country agents or providers what currency they would prefer, either bank transfer or cash (Note: many countries will not accept Scottish or Northern Irish notes). Check on the availability of ATMs and their reliability.

2.15 Agents and support

Having the support of an in-country agent can help save time and ensure that the expedition runs smoothly. They can put into place much of what has been discussed so far. Alternatively, it can be possible to travel to a country and make all your own arrangements after you arrive. Getting the right agent who will provide all the services that you require in the way in which you require them is crucial to a successful expedition. Make sure the agreement for services is agreed, written down and if necessary signed by both parties.

If you are able to recce the route or visit the country prior to the trip it may be possible to

FIGURE 2.16 MOROCCAN GUIDE   Photo: Outlook Expeditions

meet with the agents to help ensure they can provide all that is required.

Be aware that in some countries the answer to any question is what they think you want to hear rather than the truth since the host's aim is to please. Check that what you have asked for is being provided.

Agents can usually organise:
- accommodation
- in-country transport and flights
- trekking support – cooks, mules, porters
- tents
- local guides and sirdars – best if they speak English
- emergency back-up – check to find out what they would do
- additional activities such as rafting.

Personal recommendation is by far the best way of choosing the right agent. However if this is not possible try and contact a few different companies, look at their websites, and compare prices and services offered. Ask about the training and experience of the guides and whether they can provide any profiles and references. Some countries will have a programme of training and assessment and providers may adhere to a national or international standard.

2.16 Your support team

The support team may be made up of guides/ sirdars, cooks, porters, muleteers and a variety of animals, horses, mules, donkeys, yaks, etc. While their main role is to ensure the smooth running of your expedition you also have a duty of care to them.

Find out what are the local rules and guidance on loads and how heavy they may be for human or animal transport. Take an interest in your porters; ensure that they have adequate footwear and clothing for the journey on which you are embarking. Make sure that all animals are well treated.

Be aware that your support team may be as new to the route or area as you are. For example, many porters in Nepal are not mountain people like the Sherpas. They come from the lowlands to earn money and will often not acclimatise any better or quicker than your own party.

2.17 Tipping

At the end of a trek it is traditional to show appreciation for the services supplied by tipping the team. Find out what is custom and practice

Leading young people

When leading teams of young people, there are a number of additional responsibilities a leader needs to consider. With any group that you lead you have a duty of care but this is increased when adding the extra responsibility of working with under 18s. Most youth groups are led under the umbrella of a school or a voluntary, charitable or commercial organisation such as the Scouts, British Schools Exploring Society or a Commercial Trekking Company. If you are working as a leader you will have to undergo an enhanced Criminal Records Bureau (CRB) check. The expedition should only take place with the informed consent of each youngster's parents or guardian. You may also find that you are working with teachers or leaders from that organisation as part of a wider leader team. The accompanying staff would have a key pastoral role as they would probably know the youngsters well while the expedition leader would have the key roll in ensuring that the expedition programme is well managed as safely as possible. Aware-ness of additional rules and guidance for the organisation or school you may be working with is also important, as is an awareness of child protection good practice.

Photo: Nigel Williams

so that you do not under or over tip. In some countries like Tanzania the 'tip' for the mountain guides and porters is expected as part of the pay package and is at set rates. It is therefore worth discussing this with your provider at the earliest stage in order to budget effectively.

In other places a good indication is to pay an extra day's wage per person per week worked. Often monies are handed over to the chief guide or sirdar who will distribute it among the team. Sometimes party members may add equipment to the pot or tip separately members of the support team they have become friendly with.

2.18 Medical

In many destinations you will require more than a standard first aid kit for your journey. You may be many days from advanced medical support. It is worth seeking out remote or wilderness medicine training courses before you leave the UK. Also speak to your GP or find a doctor who has completed the UIAA Diploma in Mountain Medicine as they will have a greater understanding of any needs you have before leaving home.

FIGURE 2.17 TREATING BLISTERS BEFORE A DAY OF TREKKING
Photo: Nigel Williams

You may find that you are not only looking after the needs of your trekking team, but also the support team as well as their animals. Local villagers may also ask you for assistance as well. Be cautious about what you take on, what you give away and the medical, cross-contamination precautions you take.

2.19 Assessing and managing risk

All ventures in the mountains carry an element of risk – this is often part of the attraction – but this risk should be assessed and the potential for participants to be harmed must be minimised.

- Have an emergency plan for each stage of the journey.
- Identify hospitals/medical centres along your route.
- Know how to call for assistance if required.
- Communication *(see Chapter 11.6 on page 157)*.
- Have emergency numbers to hand. These to include the country's emergency services and in-country agents.
- Know what services are available; is there helicopter rescue?
- Have a plan for dealing with a serious incident *(see Chapter 11.9 on page 162)* or a death *(see Chapter 11.10 on page 163)*.
- Insurance and associated repatriation cover *(see page 11 earlier in this chapter)*.

Chapter 7 Mountain hazards on page 87 highlights in more detail the necessary steps which should be taken in order to produce a risk assessment and manage the elements accordingly.

2.20 Additional activities

Many trekking expeditions add additional activities such as rafting, beach and water activities, and mountain biking. As a leader you will have a responsibility to ensure that these are delivered as well and as safely as any other part of the programme. If using third party providers such as rafting companies these should be checked out to ensure that equipment and teaching are of an acceptable standard. Check insurance details to make sure you are covered to attend these activities and that the group is covered to participate. This often prohibits doing activities on an impromptu basis. It is wise to ensure that the group leader has the competence to assess the credibility of a provider and the service they provide.

Environmental issues

LOOKING TOWARDS THE MOIRY DAM, SWITZERLAND

Photo: Bob Kinnaird

Mountains are a common sight on this planet. They make up one-fifth of the world's landscape, and provide homes to at least one-tenth of the world's people.

FIGURE 3.01 MOUNT FUJI, JAPAN
Photo: Steve Long

Two billion people depend on mountain ecosystems for most of their food, hydro-electricity, timber and minerals. About 80 per cent of our planet's fresh water originates in the mountains. Because of the pressures forced upon these eco-systems it is becoming increasingly important to protect the mountain biome.

Humans are a natural part of many eco-systems, but since the industrial revolution their influence on the earth has been disproportionate. Many environmentalists feel that the huge problems facing the world stem not just from industrialisation and population growth but also from an underlying philosophy that views the earth as a commodity rather than a community to which humans belong. While there are many truly untouched and wild places on the planet, increasingly these ecosystems are facing pressure from human activity. As soon as humans began to explore these regions their influence was exerted. This may well have been in

sympathy with the landscape to begin with; however once people begin to live and work in an area it places strains on the environment and local resources. Deforestation to provide wood for building, fencing, fuel and transport will not only change the appearance of the landscape but also the components of that particular ecosystem. Farming practices for subsistence will change the use of the land and with it the nature of what would grow and live there naturally. To this extent the landscapes we appreciate for their 'natural beauty' are often the sum total of human influence with the process continuing as time goes on. Indeed it is possible to argue that the destiny of the natural environment now rests in human hands.

Global warming is yet another factor likely to have an increasing effect in the future. Many people argue that even this process has been accelerated by human activity; either way there is no denying that it will contribute to a change in the nature of these places.

FIGURE 3.02   SKI LIFTS IN SUMMER
Photo: www.pyb.co.uk

FIGURE 3.03   ENTERING A NATIONAL PARK
Photo: John Cousins

This may well paint a sorry picture; however it is not all doom and gloom. On the positive side there is now a greater awareness of the pressures facing these environments and through positive intervention much work is underway to conserve and preserve many areas for the future. National Parks and Reserves have been set up across the world to help protect and conserve places of natural beauty. Many have been established for some time and have served as blue prints for new initiatives in developing areas. Due to ever increasing human intervention in the natural environment it is often difficult to balance the responses to conservation. Areas are often designated for conservation in order to protect what is valued, for example landform, habitat or species and are managed accordingly in order to benefit what is being protected. While this may be important in some circumstances it leaves little opportunity for nature to take its course and can often conflict with the wilderness feeling of a landscape. Conservation in many areas is also strongly influenced by cultural perspectives and the political process. Agendas are often built around what people value the most and as a result conservation priorities become politically determined. In many countries including our own there are both government and non-governmental bodies set up to oversee conservation. Many of the non-governmental bodies are charitable organisations who tend to focus their work on a particular aspect of conservation. These groups rely on charitable donations and the work of volunteers to assist with their programmes. Donating or volunteering services is often a good way to 'put something back' and add another dimension to any trekking trip.

It is undeniable that trekking has had a significant impact on the environment, the culture and the economy of certain countries with effects both negative and positive. Indeed the opinions of experts vary regarding the extent of damage done due to trekking. However, in the last decade awareness of the problems has been raised, and solutions are being found that are already benefiting the environment and local communities.

In many countries trekking has developed into a major industry; in Nepal it is now regarded as the single most important force in their economy. Many of its schools, hospitals and new infrastructure have been built with investment derived from tourism.

Many people search for negative aspects of the trekking/tourism industry before beginning to understand and balance the benefits. Understanding the nature of our impact on the places we choose to visit is the starting point for considering how we might have a more positive effect. The nature of our impact when trekking can be divided into three categories.

- Cultural
- Economic
- Environmental

FIGURE 3.04   HISTORIC SANCTUARY OF MACHU PICCHU, UNESCO WORLD HERITAGE SITE   Photo: Mike Rosser

3.1 Cultural impact

One of the greatest attractions of trekking for many people is the opportunity it provides to meet and interact with a wide variety of people and cultures. Longer treks and expeditions allow for a more prolonged immersion in the country, leaving you with a deeper understanding of people and their cultures. These interactions and experiences are often very profound and live long in the memory, helping us to broaden our view on the world and maybe evaluate the way in which we lead our lives.

In many countries day to day life has remained unchanged and has managed to evolve independently of 'Western' influences. There is no denying that the West is a technologically advanced society; however its superiority over less developed cultures does not necessarily extend beyond this.

Many things are done differently in these countries but this does not make the methods any less valid and in some cases they may be better. When visiting most countries nowadays it is often very easy to see the western influences and while these may have a positive effect on the local people and culture it is worth remembering that we are only guests and should therefore think carefully about how we can minimise impact and influence during our stay.

- **Dress decently:** dress standards are important in many cultures and are often overlooked by visitors. While men may go around without a shirt on in the West this is considered indecent in certain countries. For women, dress codes will vary from liberal to conservative. Dressing modestly is likely to attract far less attention and cause less offence.

FIGURE 3.05   NIGHT TIME MARKET SCENE IN MARRAKECH   Photo: Mike Rosser

FIGURE 3.06 DRESSED APPROPRIATELY FOR IN-COUNTRY EXPEDITION SHOPPING Photo: Louise Turner

Being dressed in a culturally acceptable way often gains you greater respect among the local people.

- **Respect people's right to privacy:** ask people before taking their photograph and be considerate when looking for subjects. Religious ceremonies in some cultures are bright exuberant affairs, perfect subjects for recording on film; however this may be considered as an insult.
- **Don't flaunt your wealth:** in many developing countries even the poorest trekker is considered to be wealthy. Demonstrations of wealth often only attract further attention. Try not to leave valuables lying around as this is further evidence that you have so much money you can afford to replace them.
- **Respect religious customs and traditions:** there are often religious customs and traditions

that are important to respect. Research into this aspect of any trip helps to avoid actions that could be classed as insult to your hosts. Remember, many countries have a very diverse range of cultures and religions; customs and traditions can vary from valley to valley or even village to village.

- **Take an interest:** express an interest in what people are doing and try to learn about their way of life. These are often good opportunities to share experiences and may highlight that things are not as rosy in the West as some might believe.
- **Language:** while this can often be thought of as a barrier, learning a few words in the local language will greatly enhance your visit; apart from being respectful and polite it will be much appreciated and often helps to break the ice.

3.2 Economic impact

In many of the popular areas the initial effect of trekking was to increase the prices of commodities. In the short term this creates problems, particularly in developing areas where subsistence is the way of life. People become more willing to sell scarce commodities to passing trekkers. It has been shown that this is a stage in a long development process and as demand increases so to does production where previously there was no advantage to producing more. This begins to create work and stimulate the local economy benefiting the inhabitants and

FIGURE 3.07 SHERPA MEMORIALS IN NEPAL   Photo: Iain Peter

FIGURE 3.08 NEPALESE PORTER   Photo: Mal Creasey

the wider community. There are ways in which
anyone trekking can contribute positively to the
local economy.

FIGURE 3.09 BUYING LOCAL PRODUCE IN NEPAL
Photo: Mal Creasey

- *Spend money locally:* try to use local facilities, shops, hotels, lodges and people (guides
  and porters).
- *Employ local people:* there may be occasions
  when transport or logistics are required. By
  using local trekking companies and recognised guides the income you provide them with
  is more likely to stay in the local economy.
  You should take responsibility for your
  support team's welfare whilst they work for
  you. Before hiring any staff, make sure they
  will be paid a fair wage and check they have
  the necessary experience and equipment.
  If using a trekking company they should
  also have adequate rescue procedures and
  insurance cover. When employing porters it
  is important to check that the weight of any
  loads is acceptable. *The International
  Porter Protection Group* suggests a maximum load weight of 30kg.
- *Don't bargain for food and lodging:* in many
  places prices are fixed and in most cases
  reasonable. In some countries it may be the
  custom to barter for items, in others it could
  be seen as an insult. Try to do your research
  beforehand and budget for the prices quoted
  as opposed to the deal you think you might be
  able to strike.

- *Don't give to beggars:* in many places this
  has become a problem and is exacerbated by
  well meaning tourists. Embarrassed at the
  disparity in wealth between their own country
  and the destination they have given money and
  belongings in good faith thinking they were
  helping. In most cases the opposite is true and
  this only serves to foster a dependency on the
  attitude of visitors and encourage further
  begging. In some places it is possible to earn
  more through this practice than seeking out
  regular employment. So much so that more
  ingenious ways are being developed to help the
  unwary trekker part with their money. It can
  be hard to judge how genuine a claim is.
  Remember you don't have to give anything.
- *Support community projects:* one of the
  best ways to make a positive impact is to help
  support community projects. This may be
  through financial donation or by physically
  helping out in some way. Either way make
  sure that any time and money is well spent
  and that it will contribute to projects that
  have longevity for the local communities (do
  what you can to ensure that the money ends
  up where you intended).

FIGURE 3.10   COMMUNITY PROJECT IN MOROCCO

Photo: Mike Rosser

3.3 Environmental impact

We all have a duty to think about our impact on the places we visit. Trips can take on an extra dimension by thinking about how we can make a positive contribution to conserving an area for the future. It may be unrealistic to build a new school or replant a whole forest; however the small actions taken when behaving responsibly, if passed onto future travellers and generations, are often the best way to insure a long term positive impact. Trekking responsibly is about promoting the activity while conserving the environment, and respecting other people's places and ways of life. It should enable local people to benefit and help them to realise that conservation can improve their own standards of living.

There are some simple steps that can be taken to help minimise our environmental impact and insure we make this positive contribution for the future.

- **Littering:** litter generated by trekkers has long been an issue, especially in the more popular areas. Having said this, good practice and education has seen this become less of

FIGURE 3.11   COMMUNITY PROJECT

Photo: Outlook Expeditions

a problem compared to the past. Needless to say there is no excuse for dropping litter anywhere let alone in some of the most beautiful regions of the world. In most developing countries litter is a more general problem so a positive example from visiting trekking parties may go some small way towards changing attitudes. The disposal of rubbish generated during a trek needs to be considered carefully beforehand. Using local facilities provided by authorities or in villages may seem like a reasonable option in some places. In other areas this may increase the problem further by increasing the accumulation of rubbish brought from elsewhere. If it

FIGURE 3.12   BRIGHT ROCK PAINTINGS AND LARGE TREKKING GROUP NEAR SOLUKHUMBU   Photo: Mal Creasey

FIGURE 3.13   FOOTPATH EROSION IN SWITZERLAND
Photo: www.pyb.co.uk

is possible to carry it in, it should be possible to carry it out. Some National Park authorities insist on this policy and supply the necessary materials to assist with this such as rubbish bags and disposal facilities. The amount of rubbish generated on a trek can often be reduced by some prior preparation. Unnecessary packaging could be removed beforehand. It may be possible to transport certain food items in packaging that could either be burnt or recycled en route. Supported groups are often the worst for generating large amounts of rubbish and not disposing of it responsibly. Members may be careful with their litter by putting it in the bins provided at camp; however the problem of its disposal is often left to the support team of cooks and porters. Often it will be burnt or buried under a thin layer of soil, neither way being satisfactory. It has been known for the rubbish to be dumped at the most convenient point or just left at camp. The problem goes virtually unnoticed by the group members as they are often the first to depart a camp leaving the support team to clear up. As a group member or leader using a support team try to take an active role in helping with rubbish disposal so as to insure the most appropriate methods are used and the minimum amount of impact occurs.

- **_Erosion:_** a large proportion of trails are well marked paths or routes. They often provide

FIGURE 3.14 FOOTPATH IMPROVEMENTS ABOVE NAMCHE BAZAAR   Photo: Mal Creasey

essential communication between towns and villages for the local inhabitants and many routes have historical or religious significance. Often they are the best and only option for passage and it therefore becomes inevitable that with an increase in 'traffic' there comes an increase in erosion. Having said this where a path exists it is important to follow it in order to prevent further erosion and protect fragile habitats. Trekkers can help to reduce this kind of erosion by resisting the temptation to walk on edges of the paths. This is understandable when the path is muddy or stony; however it removes vegetation, allowing the soil to wash away and the path to grow steadily wider. Similarly, following the zigzags of a path in descent and ascent, rather than cutting corners, reduces the gullying that can destroy whole sections of path. When walking on paths or going 'off road' the choice of footwear can make a difference. Lightweight boots or even approach shoes will have relatively little impact compared to heavier stiffer boots. Obviously the choice will largely depend on the nature of the terrain and experience of the individual; however some consideration may help to reduce the impact (trek/ski poles also have an impact).

- **Toilet:** if a toilet is provided it makes sense to use it, but there will be times when the call of nature will need to be answered in the absence of proper facilities. Much has been written about disposing of human waste; however the method will largely depend on the environment. While burying waste is the preferred option, in some terrain this may not be possible. To bury any waste dig a hole at least 15cm deep and at least 50m from any water source and as far from footpaths or buildings as possible to avoid contamination. Toilet paper can also be buried or burnt but either way it should not be left on show. An alternative approach is to carry out all toilet waste and dispose of this on return to civilisation. A suitably tough container will be needed as well as a reliable disposal system back at base. Otherwise the risks to hygiene will outweigh the benefits to the environment. National Parks operating a carry out policy often provide all the necessary materials and facilities to assist with this.

- **Water:** washing, whether of self, clothes or pots and pans should never be done directly into a water course, even if biodegradable detergents are used. Apart from potential hygiene issues given the quality of the water in some places, it is far better to use a pot for washing and dispose of the dirty water away from the bank.

- **Fauna and flora:** try not to disturb the wildlife you encounter. In alpine areas above the tree line plants and animals battle to

FIGURE 3.15   COOKING ON AN OPEN FIRE
Photo: Outlook Expeditions

survive in a harsh environment. The unwary trekker with big boots walking off the path can easily disturb the soil and plants leaving scars that may never heal. Many people feel compelled to leave food for the local animals; however this merely serves to encourage vermin and unnatural behaviours. In some popular places this has caused issue with animals becoming reliant on 'tit bits' from travellers to the extent they have become pests.

- *Fires:* ideally trekkers should refrain from lighting fires even though this may be the most convenient way to cook, particularly on an extended trip where carrying large amounts of fuel is difficult. While consumption of firewood by trekkers is very small in some places it can be concentrated along popular trails and therefore have an impact on a local resource. Some Park authorities have now banned the use of open fires for this reason. If fires are essential ensure the fuel is used efficiently and that they are kept small to reduce damage. Never leave them unattended and make sure they are completely extinguished after use.
- *Camping:* where possible always seek permission before camping next to a house or habitation. In-country providers or guides will provide advice on permissions and costs.

FIGURE 3.16   WASHING IN THE ONLY WATER SOURCE?
Photo: Iain Peter

It may be valuable to establish these prices in advance and if necessary write them down in the form of an agreement with your provider. When camping close to a village in certain countries you will need to seek the permission from a village elder. Try to minimise the impact while in camp and ensure you leave the camp as you found it. In the case of some sites on popular trails this may involve tidying

FIGURE 3.17   BRIGHTLY COLOURED TREKKERS EN ROUTE FOR TOUBKAL   Photo: Peter Stacey

FIGURE 3.18   BALTI PORTERS COOKING ON WOOD
Photo: Iain Peter

up after other users. National Parks often have codes of conduct relating to camping to help minimise the impact on the local environment and maintain access for the future.

- *Aesthetic pollution:* while it can be very difficult to blend in completely, an awareness of our aesthetic impact will help to reduce the noise and visual pollution we might create.

3.4 The Trekkers' Code

The UIAA and other charitable organisations such as Community Action Nepal and the American Leave No Trace movement have designed guidelines and codes for trekking behaviour. These serve as a good guide to responsible trekking and help to summarise this particular chapter.

- Do not leave litter
- Consider sanitation carefully
- Do not pollute water courses
- Stick to trails to help prevent erosion and protect fragile habitats
- Minimise impact on fauna and flora
- Consider carefully the use of any fuel – deforestation is a problem in some communities
- Use established campsites where possible
- Buy local food and produce – support the local economy
- Employ local people
- Support community projects
- Respect culture, traditions and religions
- Respect people's privacy – be sensitive when taking photographs
- Do not encourage begging
- Encourage everyone to adopt conservation measures
- Enjoy the peace and quiet

FIGURE 3.19   LOOKING TOWARDS AMA DABLAM   Photo: Iain Peter

3.5 Environmental audit

It is only the expeditions that never go beyond the drawing board that have no impact whatsoever. It is important to be realistic about the nature of the impact we may have if we are to take any minimising actions. In the same way as we conduct a risk assessment prior to a trip we should also allocate time to conduct an environmental risk assessment. Using a similar process to the one outlined in this it is possible to identify areas where we may have an environmental impact and to then put in place measures which will mitigate the effects and help reduce this level of impact. By conducting this assessment in the early stages of planning it allows thought to be given to this issue and plans to be made to increase the chance of success with a more minimal impact approach. With large groups, appointing an environmental monitor to oversee the implementation of any such plans will also help to ensure the expedition is conducted in such a way as to reduce its impact.

In summary it is worth remembering that our impact while trekking extends beyond footpath erosion and litter, and only with a planned integrated approach that recognises the potential influences we may have on our destinations will it be possible to truly minimise the impact.

FIGURE 3.20   MOUNT COOK LILIES   Photo: Mo Laurie

Leader's Information

Environmental education

As a leader of any group in the hills we have the privilege of commanding a very influential position. The ability to educate and enthuse people about the environment they walk through can be extremely rewarding and often adds a new dimension to the day for both the leader and the group. Few leaders will be specialists in such subjects as geography, biology or history but this should not inhibit them from sharing their interests and enthusiasms with others. Everyone has something to offer and it's a sorry leader who has no interests at all. Researching the natural history of an area before departure is often a great way to begin the process of educating people about the environment. It can often spark various interests among group members providing individuals with a focus for the trip, whether it's trying to find a rare plant or an ancient settlement. The most important skill to develop, however, is not identifying species or rock types but simply noticing the detail in your surroundings, and having noticed it being able to bring it to the attention of the group. People learn in different ways and are attracted to different things. Something of interest to one person may seem mundane and boring to another. However using sights, sounds, smells, textures and even tastes it is possible to engage

Photo: www.pyb.co.uk

people in a more interactive way with the environment. With passion and enthusiasm it is possible to inspire people and awaken their curiosity for further knowledge. It's often the act of noticing and appreciating that is important, for not only will this enhance the pleasure of the day, but may lead to a more caring attitude towards the environment in the future. Interest in the small detail will often lead toward fostering a more caring attitude for the wider environment. Caring for the mountain environment not only modifies behaviour on it, but also leads to a more widespread concern for the issues faced in mountain regions across the globe. The potential influence of the leader in promoting awareness and fostering a concerning attitude, particularly with young groups, cannot be overstated.

FIGURE 3.21   SWISS COW

Photo: Helen Barnard

ATLAS TREKKING

Photo: Outlook Expeditions

Staying healthy

Travelling abroad raises a number of issues. For many the primary concern will be how to stay healthy, especially when deprived of all the modern trappings we are used to in the developed world, such as clean water, fresh food and good sanitation facilities.

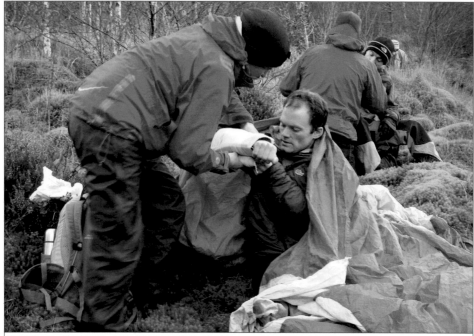

FIGURE 4.01 PRACTICAL FIRST AID TRAINING IN ACTION   Photo: www.pyb.co.uk

Seeking expert medical advice and treatment abroad when faced with illness or injury can be daunting, particularly when there is a language barrier to overcome. Good preparation and research beforehand can often prevent problems and help solve them more efficiently should they arise.

have a combination of the two. Medical expertise may vary and the patient could have to travel a considerable distance to receive specialist care. Before travelling spend time researching the availability of medical care in the destination country. It is important that travel insurance for the trip reflects the level of risk and cost of medical care *(see **Chapter 2** on page 7).*

4.1 Research

The internet provides invaluable advice with a multitude of blogs on travellers' experiences. Travel guides such as *Lonely Planet* and *Rough Guides* provide a lot of information as do the NHS and WHO websites on potential illnesses.

4.2 Medical care

The provision of medical care will vary from country to country. In some countries, hospitals and medical treatment will be provided by the state and in others it will be private. Some countries

4.3 Training and advice

As identified in the previous chapter, attending a remote area first aid course could prove invaluable if planning to travel in remote areas or where self rescue and/or self treatment is the only option. While this chapter provides information on many of the potential issues, it is not exhaustive, hence the reason to seek additional advice from a qualified and experienced medical practitioner or a doctor involved in the UIAA Diploma in Mountain Medicine.

The World Health Organisation (WHO) and the FCO are invaluable sources of information when planning any kind of overseas trip. Their websites are full of useful information for travellers.

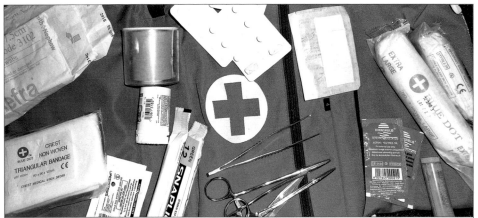

FIGURE 4.03 A PACKED MEDICAL KIT   Photo: John Cousins

4.4 Immunisations

It is recommended to consult a doctor or travel health professional for the latest information on immunisations. This should be done a minimum of four months before the start of the trip as some vaccines require several injections.

The vaccines required will depend on the following:

- existing vaccination status
- the countries to be visited
- the duration in contact with local people
- the standard of accommodation
- the anticipated activity

Some countries require vaccination certificates as entry requirements; check with the relevant embassy before travel.

Essential
- Tetanus
- Polio
- Typhoid
- Hepatitis A

Consider
- Diphtheria
- Yellow fever
- Japanese encephalitis
- Rabies
- Hepatitus B (DH)
- Cholera

Malaria and dengue fever are diseases spread by mosquitos. Depending on your area of travel,

 Leader's Information

Medical declarations
Sometimes clients travelling with trekking companies do not declare medical issues or medication for fear they will not be allowed to go on the trek. Leaders must not therefore assume that all medical conditions have been written down and should do everything to encourage participants to declare all necessary information.

preventative medication for malaria should be considered. Currently there is no preventative medication for dengue fever. In both cases avoid getting bitten by using insect repellent every six hours and covering exposed flesh with clothing (they can still bite through light clothing). Use mosquito nets and insect spray at night and avoid areas where they breed such as stagnant water (see **Chapter 7 Trekking hazards** on page 85).

4.5 Travelling with medication

It is worth considering a medical check-up as part of the preparation for a trekking trip, especially if travelling to altitude. This is even more relevant for individuals with pre-existing medical conditions, such as diabetes or asthma. If medication is required, then it is important to ensure that an adequate supply is available for the duration of the trip, plus extra as contingency

FIGURE 4.04 WALKING IN THE UK, ASCENDING SNOWDON   Photo: John Cousins

FIGURE 4.05 CARRYING A HEAVY RUCKSACK
Photo: Helen Barnard

Ensure there is sufficient cleaning solution for contact lenses as it is can be difficult to source in some countries.

If travelling to remote areas or to developing countries consider taking an intravenous (IV) and suturing kit as the availability of sterile needles may be limited; also providing your own reduces the risk of infections and illnesses.

4.6 Physical preparation

Ideally, anyone going trekking should arrive already physically fit, having taken the time to train and prepare their bodies for the extra demands of such a holiday. Planning ahead and setting a training programme that progressively improves fitness will help to prepare for the trip.

To increase the chances of success and sustaining a new fitness regime, the training programme needs to revolve around work and family commitments. It is important to look at one's lifestyle and find changes that are not too onerous. Examples of this might include walking to work instead of driving, cycling to the shops or walking to collect the children from school. Build into the week occasions when exercise can regularly be taken, such as before work, after work or at the weekend. Maintaining a regular

(dispersed among the group). Check that the medication is not one of the controlled drugs in the country you are visiting. In many countries, carrying drugs and painkillers may cause legal problems that could result in a prison sentence or worse. Carry copies of pre-scriptions and a letter from the doctor detailing any medication.

If an individual wears contact lenses or glasses, take spares and a copy of the lens prescription.

training day or days will increase the likelihood of exercise actually taking place – three times a week should be sufficient if well thought-out.

The fitness requirements for trekking are predominantly **strength** and **endurance**, with skill components of **balance** and *flexibility*. These are the areas of fitness that everyone should aim to improve over time in preparation for a trip.

4.6.1 Strength
When trekking we are constantly working against our own body weight, the weight of a rucksack and gravity via the slope angle. While this does not require maximum strength, it is important to condition the muscles to the stresses and strains placed on the body during such an activity in order to avoid early fatigue or injury.

4.6.2 Endurance
Endurance or stamina can often be described as the ability to keep going with a movement or activity for a relatively long period of time. Trekking, particularly at altitude, is reliant on effective oxygen uptake to meet the demands of the working muscles. Referred to as aerobic capacity it is dependant upon efficient respiratory, cardiac and vascular systems. Activities such as walking, running, cycling, swimming and rowing are all good at developing aerobic capacity and improving endurance, plus they will help condition and build strength.

4.6.3 Balance
Balance is the ability to control the body's position; a person is balanced when their centre of gravity is over their area of support. The ability to balance requires a combination of information from various parts of the body; sensory organs in the inner ear, the eyes, plus receptors in the muscles and tendons. Trekking places greater demand on dynamic balance as walkers need to retain their balance while in motion. The use of walking poles can help individuals on more difficult ground by increasing the number of points of contact. However the over-reliance on poles may lead to a loss in the body's natural ability to balance in these situations.

4.6.4 Flexibility
Improving flexibility is an important element in injury prevention. Research confirms there is a correlation between muscular tightness and

FIGURE 4.06   FELL RUNNING   Photo: John Cousins

increased risk of muscle strain. Stretching to improve flexibility will over time be beneficial to a mountain walker, particularly if they encounter uneven ground or short rock steps. Stretching can be incorporated into a warm up and warm down routine as mentioned in the basic training programme below or as a standalone session.

4.7 Training programmes

The variety of training programmes available can be overwhelming with everything from tailor-made courses from personal trainers to 'off the shelf' sessions from magazines and websites. Consider carefully your needs and the amount of time available before making any decision. Seeking professional advice from a trainer or local gym may also provide some useful ideas. Before embarking on any training programme visit a doctor for a medical check-up and further advice. Pre-existing injuries or medical issues could cause problems if the training programme is not properly managed.

A basic training programme should include the following principles.

4.7.1 Specificity
The activity used to increase the fitness level needs to reflect the type of activity the person is training for. As mentioned previously trekking requires endurance, therefore the training activity needs to replicate this and be of a low intensity and long duration.

FIGURE 4.07   STRETCHING EXERCISES: **A** THIGH STRETCH   **B** CALF STRETCH   **C** NECK STRETCH   **D** SHOULDER STRETCH   **E** HAMSTRING STRETCH

Photos: www.pyb.co.uk

4.7.2 Progressive overload

The cardiovascular system and muscles increase their capacity for exercise if training is progressive and overloaded. The training programme must stress the system above the level to which it is accustomed to have any improvement on fitness. For example, a mountain walker needs to progressively increase the length of walks undertaken, height ascended and descended, increase walking speed or increase the weight of rucksacks carried.

4.7.3 Reversibility

When training is stopped for a significant period of time, the level of fitness is reversed. It is suggested that those who have undergone a relatively short period of training exhibit the fastest rates of reversibility, whereas those who have trained for long periods of time appear to be able to sustain their fitness for a longer period.

4.7.4 Variety

The lack of motivation to train over time is often caused by the lack of variety of exercise. Individuals are more likely to maintain their fitness regime by varying the activity each week and finding a way of enjoying it.

4.7.5 Warm up and warm down

Although strictly not a principle of training, a warm up and warm down play an important role in any exercise. A training session should include a warm up, the work out and then the warm down. The purpose of the warm up is to raise the temperature and increase blood flow to the muscles and the body, increase alertness and reduce the risk of injury. It is also recommended that stretching should be included in this phase.

The range of movement in the warm up should reflect the range of movement specific to the activity about to be undertaken. For example, footballers should include running forwards, backwards and changing direction, and kicking the ball.

The warm down at the end of a training session is essential to decrease body temperature and remove waste products from the working muscles. Static stretches are more appropriate at the end of the session as they help the muscles to relax, realign fibres and re-establish their normal range of movement.

The illustrations *(see Figure 4.07)* are of the range of stretches useful after an arduous walk to an Alpine hut. It is important, particularly on multi-day trips, to include warming up and warming down as part of the daily routine. Stiff and sore muscles will ultimately lead to a reduction in performance over time. Delayed Onset Muscle Soreness (DOMS) occur through overuse of underprepared muscles. RICE (Rest, Ice, Compression and Elevation) are effective treatments, though not all at the same time!

Even the journey to a foreign country can present issues with regards health. The stress of busy airports, lack of food and sleep, dehydration due to air conditioning on the plane are factors that may affect the body's immune system, making it more susceptible to problems on arrival in-country. Therefore plan the journey carefully, make sure you have adequate food and drink available, try to sleep and rest when possible plus factor in some recovery time at the destination.

FIGURE 4.08   MORNING STRETCHING SESSION BEFORE A DAYS TREKKING IN GREENLAND   Photo: Nigel Williams

4.8 Travel sickness

Travel or motion sickness is a common condition faced by many people and can have lasting effects after arrival in-country.

The following can help to reduce the chance of travel sickness.

- Avoiding heavy meals and alcohol before travelling.
- Keeping still with eyes closed.
- Anti-sickness medicines from the pharmacist. These should be taken before travel according to the instructions so they have time to be absorbed by the body.
- Ginger or peppermint remedies. Ginger can be taken as a biscuit, tea or in crystallised form, while peppermint can be sucked as a sweet or taken as a tea.
- Acupressure. This can be applied using a wristband or by pressing your finger against the middle of the inner wrist about three finger widths above the crease where the wrist joins the hand.

FIGURE 4.09   TRYING DIFFERENT FOOD

Photo: www.pyb.co.uk

4.9 Staying healthy in-country

The key to staying healthy in-country is to think carefully about eating, drinking and hygiene. This is important for two reasons. First to ensure sufficient energy is obtained for the activity and to reduce the risk of susceptibility to various conditions such as dehydration or hypothermia and second to avoid contact with anything that could cause illness.

4.10 Eating and drinking

Eating and drinking adequately and safely while travelling in developing counties can be a problem and requires good planning and preparation.

4.10.1 Food

Food provides the body with energy and it is therefore important to achieve the correct balance, not only on day walks, but also on multi-day trips. Both altitude and exercise suppress appetites. The amount of calories an individual needs each day will depend on age, height, weight, the level of activity and body composition. On average, the calorie intake a woman requires is 2000 and a man 2500 calories. This amount may increase to 6000 calories or more depending on the intensity of the activity. Often on arduous expeditions calorie intake may not be sufficient and weight loss may be more of a concern. Consider doubling your calorie intake from the recommended normal levels. However be realistic about the practicalities of transporting the food and availability of time to eat it.

Proteins, carbohydrates, fats, minerals, vitamins and water are all components of a healthy diet.

- Proteins are necessary for growth, repair and maintenance of body tissues and the production of haemoglobin.
- Carbohydrates exist mainly in the form of sugars and starches and are used as a major energy source. Carbohydrates are stored in the liver and muscles as glycogen.
- Fats are a good source of slow release energy. Nutritionists recommend that fats should not exceed 25 per cent of your dietary intake, with 10 per cent being saturated fat (fats that tend to be hard at room temperature, i.e. animal fats).
- Minerals are required in small amounts to assist in a number of chemical reactions which maintain the stability of bodily functions.

FIGURE 4.10   FOOD BEING PREPARED FOR LUNCH IN ARGENTINA   Photo: Iain Peter

- Vitamins are essential for metabolic reactions within the cells and the maintenance of general health.
- Water is the main constituent of blood and is the medium for transporting nutrients around the body. It is required in urine to remove waste products and as sweat for regulating body temperature.

A balanced diet may be difficult to achieve on a trek. Where possible a third of the meal should consist of starchy foods such as pasta, rice and potatoes. The body converts these complex carbohydrates into glycogen to provide energy, thereby delaying the onset of exhaustion. It is important to avoid sugary foods and drinks as they release energy too quickly. A sudden rise in sugar levels leads to over production of insulin and is followed by a rapid reduction in blood sugar level.

The availability of fresh fruit and vegetables will also be limited, especially at higher altitudes and in remote areas. It is recommended that another third of your meal should consist of fruit and vegetables, with five portions eaten per day. Take every opportunity to buy fresh food when travelling through towns and villages; it can provide a welcome respite from packaged food and boost moral. Vitamin supplements on extended trips are useful to compensate for the lack of available fresh fruit and vegetables.

Reduce the amount of saturated fat in the meal. It may make the meal more appetising especially at altitude but it is slow to digest.

FIGURE 4.11   FRESH PRODUCE AT A MARKET IN MARRAKECH   Photo: Helen Barnard

Dehydrated food may be necessary to keep weight down for transportation; however it does tend to have a high salt content. Hence, it is important not to add additional salt and to stay hydrated.

A good solution to maintaining a blood sugar level is to eat little and often throughout the day; grazing as opposed to troughing. Large meals often cause indigestion and the blood is diverted to the stomach rather than the working muscles making walking harder. Try to snack between 20–60 grams of carbohydrate every hour.

Coping with different dietary needs on expeditions can be difficult depending on the country. Local people may not understand the concept of being vegetarian, vegan or lactose intolerant. This may result in the poor provision of food.

FIGURE 4.12   WATER HYGIENE AT CAMP   Photo: Iain Peter

FIGURE 4.13   DRINKING FROM AN ALPINE WATER TROUGH   Photo: Mal Creasey

More often individuals cope by supplementing their food with produce brought from the UK.

The following points may be useful when organising your food for an expedition.

- The majority of your energy will come from carbohydrates (60–70 per cent). The food should be easy to carry, cook and eat.
- The average portion of carbohydrate for an adult per meal is 100 grams. Increase this quantity if going to altitude, undertaking physically demanding activity or in a cold environment.
- Take food you really like and have plenty of variety. At altitude you rarely feel hungry, but having your favourite food may provide more temptation to eat regularly.
- Give some thought to the way you package and transport food during the expedition. Mixing fuel and food in the same container is not recommended; even a small amount of fuel leaking into the container can contaminate all the food. Disaster if it's your chocolate stash!
- Removing excess packaging will not only save on weight but reduce the amount of waste carried out at the end of the trip.
- Transfer foodstuffs such as herbs and spices into re-useable plastic containers.
- Research your destination and find out which animals are likely to want to eat your food.

Bears, insects, vermin and birds all are quite partial to human food given the chance.

- Dividing up the food into daily portions before departure saves time on the trip. This reduces the chance of all of one particular food type being spoilt or lost in transit. It also helps you work out how much you need and therefore avoids carrying too much spare food.
- Have a contingency plan for delays – a few extra days food may be important if your schedule doesn't go to plan.

4.10.2 Food poisoning

Staying healthy and free from stomach upsets; diarrhoea and food poisoning can be a challenge especially in developing countries where food hygiene procedures may be poor. All too often trekkers suffer from travellers' diarrhoea, 'Delhi Belly' or 'Kathmandu Quickstep', and are therefore unable to travel anywhere for a few days. This may create logistical problems, particularly when following a tight schedule, and from the individual's point of view it will be disappointing and uncomfortable. The leader will need to consider the impact on a team and the itinerary if an individual is ill, hospitalised and even if they need evacuation. When travelling to altitude, suffering from diarrhoea and staying hydrated can be difficult, and may require additional medical help.

FIGURE 4.14 A GROUP SHELTERING FROM THE SUN   Photo: www.pyb.co.uk

When preparing food ensure that raw meat is kept away from other food and surfaces are regularly cleaned. Ensure there is clean water for everyone to wash their hands after visiting the toilet and always wash your hands before eating. All vegetables and fruit will need to be washed in treated water. Plates, cutlery and cups can harbour bacteria and should therefore be washed in sterilising fluid before use.

Following the principle of 'boil it, cook it, peel it or forget it' will make all the difference in an attempt to keep free from illness.

4.10.3 Drinking

Regular and plentiful water intake helps regulate the body's temperature control and prevent heat-related illnesses. At altitude and in cold environments, dehydration is a real risk due to increased breathing rate (vapour is lost each time you breathe out) and the lack of motivation to drink in cold conditions. Vomiting and diarrhoea can also cause fluid loss. Dehydration will affect both mental and physical performance of an individual.

It is important to set off for a mountain day fully hydrated. Drink a minimum of 2 litres during the trek and then continue to re-hydrate in the evening. The amount of water necessary per day to stay hydrated will vary according to the intensity of the activity and the climatic conditions. Alcohol should be avoided and drinks that contain caffeine should be limited as they only serve to increase the amount of water loss through urination as they have a diuretic effect.

Regular hourly drink stops during the day should become routine, and trekkers should monitor their urine output as an indication to whether they are hydrated or not. Clear and copious urine output needs to be achieved. Team members should be encouraged to report on their level of hydration. Thirst is an indication of critical dehydration and therefore individuals should avoid the feeling of thirst through proper hydration management. Once again the 'little and often' approach to drinking serves as a good solution to this problem.

The use of hydration bags for drinking should be carefully managed particularly with youth groups. From a leader's point of view it can be difficult to see how much the group are drinking, and often they are less than careful where the hose ends up when they place their rucksack on the ground i.e. lying on the dirty floor. An old film canister can be used to protect the nozzle from any contamination.

Excessive sweating will affect the body's balance of electrolytes and levels of sodium chloride (salt) and consequently cause muscle cramps. To replace the essential salts and electrolytes, consume either a specialist isotonic drink (often hard to find in developing countries), or use simple oral rehydration solutions diluted in water. As an alternative, add a level teaspoon of salt and four teaspoons of sugar to each litre of water.

With a large trekking group it can be very difficult for the porters and cook teams to supply enough fluid for every client. The availability of fuel and time will be limited, and hence in these situations it is worth each person assuming responsibility for treating their own water.

4.11 Water treatment

Waterborne diseases are common in all parts of the world where there is poor hygiene and sanitation. The most common source of exposure to disease for trekkers is ingestion of contaminated drinking water and food. It therefore becomes important to treat water and food carefully before eating and drinking to avoid exposure to any harmful bacteria or viruses.

FIGURE 4.15   BOILING WATER FOR TOMORROW'S DRINKS BOTTLES   Photo: John Cousins

FIGURE 4.16   BOILING WATER AT ALTITUDE
Photo: Iain Peter

4.11.1 Treatment
On occasions the treatment of water should be considered as a two stage process that requires the water to be filtered and then sterilised.

4.11.2 Filtration
Filtration involves clarifying the water to remove dirt, glacial till, leaves and other rubbish. Ideally, the water source should be carefully selected and free from obvious contaminates.

Where possible the stream should be fast flowing and every effort made to check up-stream for habitation (campsite, village or animals) and other potential sources of contamination. Filtering water through either a tightly woven canvas such as a Millbank bag, a pair of tights, or a t-shirt are all effective methods of removing sediment. Otherwise leave the water to settle and so allow the sediment to sink to the bottom and then decant the clear water.

Once clear, the water then needs to be sterilised. This will kill the bacteria and viruses that are harmful and can be done by either boiling or using chemicals.

4.11.3 Boiling
Boiling water and then allowing it to cool is the most effective way of killing all pathogens. A vigorous boil for at least one minute is sufficient. However, boiling may not be a practical option due to fuel, time or technical constraints.

4.11.4 Boiling at altitude
The temperature at which water boils decreases with altitude. A 'rule of thumb' is that it boils 1°C less for every 300m of altitude. Bringing water to a rolling boil at any altitude will do the job. The latest research suggests that water boiling with bubbles for at least one minute kills all pathogens except Hepatitis A therefore making the water safe. Hepatitis A is very rare at high alti-tude and most people are vaccinated against it.

4.11.5 Chemical sterilisation
Until recently Iodine and Chlorine were the two most commonly used chemicals for the sterilisation of water. The sale and use of iodine in drinking water has been banned by European law since October 2009 due to the possible side effects. However iodine may still be available outside the EU.

Iodine is reasonably effective against most pathogens, but is not effective against Cryptosporidium. The effectiveness of the treatment depends on the water temperature and concentration of suspected pathogens. The standard dose is five drops of two per cent iodine tincture in one litre of water for a minimum of one hour contact time. Cold water and suspected Giardia requires greater concentration of iodine and longer treatment time.

It is important that the water is prepared according to the instructions and should not be given to those with thyroid problems, pregnant women and children under five. Prolonged use over three months is also not recommended. Any flavouring or neutralising should be added to water only after sufficient contact time has elapsed. If the taste is unpleasant, try treating it the night before; by morning the taint will be minimal.

Chlorine is effective at killing most bacteria, but is less effective for viruses and cysts. Similarly to iodine, chlorine will require greater concentrations and treatment time if Giardia is suspected and the water is cold. Chlorine is not effective against Cryptosporidium or some other parasites.

4.11.6 Portable filtration devices and pumps

Many trekkers prefer to use one of the many filtration devices and pumps available. Some devices filter the water through a ceramic or carbon filter and then treat the water chemically. Unfortunately, the filtration process eventually leads to the pores becoming blocked, requiring dismantling, cleaning and reassembling. Careful handling of the pump is required as a broken or cracked ceramic filter can compromise the pump's ability to work properly. In cold conditions, if a used ceramic filter freezes it will break.

The pore size of the filter is important and the most effective devices have a pore size 1-micron or less. This size will remove Giardia, Cryptosporidium and other protozoa. Some filters may not remove all viruses and therefore the water will still require further chemical treatment or boiling to be safe.

4.11.7 UV light

The ultraviolet radiation renders the viruses, bacteria and protozoa sterile and therefore unable to reproduce and cause harm to humans.

UV light treatment is effective in the prevention of Cryptosporidium. The range of UV water treatment systems available is huge and good light-weight products are available for carrying on treks. To be most effective, water treated by UV light systems needs to be filtered first.

On the downside these devices are expensive and use a lot of batteries; there is also no way to be sure that they have worked.

FIGURE 4.17   WATER PUMP IN USE   Photo: Mo Laurie

FIGURE 4.18   A UV LIGHT PEN TREATING WATER
Photo: www.pyb.co.uk

FIGURE 4.19   DRINKING FROM A PERSONAL WATER BOTTLE   Photo: Outlook Expeditions

FIGURE 4.20   THE TOILET IS THE LAST THING TO PACK AWAY   Photo: Mike Rosser

4.12 Other sources of contamination

When travelling it is important to remain aware of the more subtle sources of contaminated water.

- Avoid fruit juice, ice cream, salads, fruit and ice cubes in drinks.
- Avoid sharing water bottles and hydration systems.
- Ensure bottled drinks are opened in front of you.

- Treat tap water with suspicion; cleaning teeth and washing food in untreated water can also cause illness.
- Keep your mouth shut in the shower – no singing!

4.13 Human waste – good practice in the outdoors

The chapter on environmental issues deals with the subject of human waste disposal. However it should be recognised at this point that dealing with human waste is a potential source of contamination and therefore needs to be considered carefully. It is paramount to maintain a good hygiene regime, for example washing hands after using the toilet to avoid any cross contamination.

4.14 Common medical conditions

- Upset stomach
- Cuts and chapped skin that heals very slowly
- Rashes

4.15 Cold

The majority of cold injuries can be avoided with the correct clothing, equipment, plus adequate food and drink. When travelling to a cold climate it is important to be familiar with the signs and symptoms of any cold related ailment encountered.

In the context of trekking, symptoms of hypothermia, dehydration, low blood sugar level, brain injury, alcohol poisoning and altitude related illnesses are all very similar. Therefore it is important to check all possibilities and consider past history and the environment when making a diagnosis.

4.15.1 Hypothermia

The normal core body temperature of a person is approximately 37°C and hypothermia occurs when this drops to below 35°C.

There are two types of hypothermia.

- **Immersion hypothermia:** a sudden drop of core temperature due to immersion in cold water.
- **Exhaustion hypothermia:** a slow and progressive drop in core temperature due to a combination of climatic conditions, insufficient or inappropriate clothing, lack of food and fluid and physical exertion.

It is likely due to the nature of trekking that exhaustion hypothermia is more common than immersion hypothermia. It is important that the symptoms of hypothermia are noticed in both those around you and in yourself. At high altitudes where the environment is cold and the days often arduous, preventing hypothermia can be a real challenge.

4.15.2 Frostbite

Frostbite is the localised freezing of skin tissue and the formation of ice crystals between the cells. This usually occurs in sub-zero temperatures, where the casualty has poor insulation, and usually affects the extremities including fingers, toes, nose and ear lobes. The risk of frostbite developing is increased by restrictive clothing, hypothermia, dehydration, exhaustion and is particularly common at altitude. The injury can be superficial or deep. The more severe cases of the latter may lead to amputation of the limb.

FIGURE 4.21   COLD TREKKING, PARANG LA, INDIA
Photo: Pete Stacey

FIGURE 4.22   THE TIME TO BE ALERT ABOUT DANGERS OF FROSTNIP – MOVING SLOWLY IN UNEXPECTED SNOW STORM AT ALTITUDE   Photo: Mal Creasey

Initially the casualty usually complains of pain followed by the loss of sensation and a wooden feeling to the affected area.

The immediate treatment for frostbite involves re-warming of the affected area. However this should only be attempted if it can be guaranteed not to re-freeze. Placing the affected area into a warm environment for approximately ten minutes and maintaining warmth by replacing wet items of clothing with dry ones will help to re-warm the affected areas. If there has been no recovery after this process, then severe frostbite should be suspected and specialist medical

Dealing with the cold

Encourage trekkers to practice taking photographs, using karabiners, etc. with gloves on prior to the trip. Ensure that cuffs, gloves and boots are loose fitting. Create a 'buddy system' to help manage equipment and to look out for signs and symptoms of hypothermia, frostbite and frostnip on each other.

Photo: Andy Cunningham and Allen Fyffe, *Winter Skills*

FIGURE 4.23   HOT TREK   Photo: Outlook Expeditions

advice should be sought. People who have suffered from frostbite in the past often complain about being more susceptible to the cold than before.

The UK Frostbite Advice Service provides excellent advice on the latest medical treatment of severe frostbite conditions via their website.

4.15.3 Frostnip

Frostnip is the superficial freezing of the skin tissue. Early identification is crucial as rapid re-warming, although painful at the time, will not lead to any permanent damage.

4.16 Heat

The daily temperature range encountered in many popular trekking destinations means that suffering from heat related problems is a real risk. The overnight temperatures may drop to freezing, but once the sun is up the daytime temperature can be extremely high leading to dehydration and hyperthermia. In humid environments these problems can be exacerbated. Such conditions can easily be avoided with careful planning. Early starts and early finishes, streams to refill water bottles, correct clothing and an appropriate route choice and distances will all help to reduce the risks.

4.16.1 Hyperthermia

An individual regulates their heat in a number of ways.

- *Vasodilatation:* increasing blood flow to the skin.
- *Sweating:* the evaporation of water from the skin.
- *Behaviour:* the removal of clothing or heat source.

The body is very intolerant of too much heat and in hot climates if the outside temperature or the severity of exercise isn't reduced this can result in heat exhaustion and the more serious heat stroke.

FIGURE 4.24   HOT GROUP TREK   Photo: Outlook Expeditions

4.16.2 Heat exhaustion

The symptoms of heat exhaustion include headaches, fatigue, muscular cramps, thirst and nausea. The treatment is simple and effective through the removal of heat by seeking shade, fanning and the removal of clothes plus the replacement of essential water, salts and electrolytes through oral rehydration sachets.

4.16.3 Heat stroke

Heat stroke is a more serious condition, where the body's ability to control heat has failed and the body's core temperature has risen above 41°C. The skin is hot and dry to touch. The increasing rise in temperature will result in further damage and there is a significant loss of the casualty's level of consciousness. Urgent evacuation of the casualty is required along with immediate surface cooling.

FIGURE 4.25   RESTING IN THE SHADE   Photo: Outlook Expeditions

FIGURE 4.26 SHERPAS WITH TOTAL SUN BLOCK Photo: Iain Peter

FIGURE 4.27 SUN HAT AND SUN CREAM
Photo: www.pyb.co.uk

4.17 Snow blindness

The intense ultraviolet light at altitude can cause painful and gritty eyes, commonly known as snow blindness, if effective sunglasses or goggles are not worn. Even on cloudy days glasses should be worn to prevent snow blindness.

Treatment for snow blindness includes rest, padding to the eyes, eye wash and painkillers. Consider carrying spare sunglasses and goggles for the trip. Improvised goggles can be made from cardboard with thin slits to look through.

4.18 Sunburn

At high altitude there are increased risks of skin damage through ultraviolet radiation from the sun. The intensity of the UV radiation is increased in snow-covered ground and any reflective terrain such as water, light rocks and boulders. Consider using a high factor sunscreen (SPF 25 or greater) and ensure that particular attention is paid to lips, nose and ears. Try to cover up with sensible clothing and hats.

4.19 Foot care

Foot care while trekking is crucial. Suffering from blisters or more serious conditions can jeopardise any trip. It can be worth taking a light-weight pair of shoes or sandals to change into at the end of the day.

FIGURE 4.28   SORE FEET BUT STILL SMILING   Photo: Outlook Expeditions

4.20 Trench foot

Trench foot is caused by prolonged exposure of the feet to low temperatures and damp conditions. It is commonly caused by damp socks and boots. The low temperatures and reduction of peripheral circulation to the extremities often results in damage to skin and nerves. This causes prickling sensations and pain with redness, blisters and swelling affecting the area. A routine each evening, cleaning, warming and drying feet will help to prevent this condition. This may also be used in the early treatment of the condition where elevating the feet will also provide some relief. In more severe cases, further treatment must be carried out by a qualified doctor (further advice is available from the UK Frostbite Advice Service).

4.21 Blisters

Although not a life threatening condition, blistered feet can be very painful and debilitating. Often new boots are bought specifically for the trip, which is why time should be spent breaking them in prior to departure.

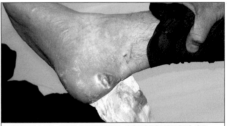

FIGURE 4.29   THE POTENTIAL CONSEQUENCES OF NOT LOOKING AFTER YOUR FEET   Photo: Nigel Williams

Gradually increase the distances walked in the new boots and progressively add more weight to a rucksack until you are satisfied that your feet will cope with long days and a heavy rucksack. Stop and cover any 'hot spots' as soon as they appear.

- Remember prevention is always better than cure.
- Ensure boots fit correctly and are broken in before the trek.
- Have a daily routine of washing, cleaning and drying your feet.
- Use a medicated foot powder.
- Wash socks at every opportunity.
- At the first signs of a blister stop and treat.
- Keep a small blister kit handy for running repairs, 'gaffer' tape can be effective in the early stages.

Trekking at altitude

Photo: Louise Turner

High altitude is said to begin at 2,500m and at this height the air is thin enough to have a noticeable effect on many people. Altitude is therefore an inevitable and in many ways desirable part of most trekking destinations, which has to be dealt by every traveller.

5.1 Altitude

All too often people accept that going to altitude involves feeling rotten for several days, with sleepless nights and headaches. Unfortunately, in the 'cash rich and time poor' society of today, people tend to push themselves too hard and therefore do not allow their body time to acclimatise. An all too familiar tale involves people travelling quickly to a destination, racing to spend a night high up in a hut to climb a substantial peak the following day and then falling ill from the altitude. Given time to properly acclimatise, being at altitude should be a safe and pleasurable experience and not something to be endured.

5.2 What is high altitude?

High altitude is defined as heights between 2500 and 3500 metres above sea level. Heights above this are defined as very high altitude (3500–5800m) and extreme altitude (above 5800m). Additionally, for a given altitude, barometric pressure is higher at the equator than the poles and is higher in summer than in winter. Therefore ascending Kilimanjaro at 5895 metres close to the equator seems easier than climbing a peak of a similar height in the southern Andes.

5.2.1 Why the effect?

With increasing altitude above sea level, air pressure decreases (the air gets 'thinner'). In simple terms, the higher a person travels, the lower the air pressure and therefore for each single breath there will be less oxygen inspired. Oxygen is required to help provide the energy to move and keep the body alive. With time the body can adapt to altitudes up to 5000 or 5500 metres. However above this height the adaptation of the body is poor and general health and physical performance progressively deteriorates.

The effect of altitude on the body begins from around 1500 to 2000 metres. Altitude illness can start to develop with rapid ascent to 2500 metres or more, with 25 per cent of travellers suffering with symptoms of acute mountain sickness (AMS).

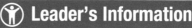

(👤) Leader's Information

Managing acclimatisation
Have regular briefings to the group about the effects of altitude. Keep a note book or diary on observations of the clients' symptoms. Provide opportunities for clients to share their anxieties and feelings in confidence.

Photo: Iain Peter

5.3 Acclimatisation

On arrival at high altitude the body adapts to the changes in oxygen levels by increasing the breathing and heart rate. Additionally, the body produces more red blood cells to increase the oxygen-carrying capacity of the blood. This increased production of red blood cells usually occurs after about four days at high altitude. The body has the ability to adjust to higher altitudes if given enough time. The process of adaptation is called acclimatisation. The rate at which each individual acclimatises is very different, so unfortunately no single rule works for everyone. Changes take time to happen; however there are good guidelines.

* From a height of 3000m, increase the sleeping height by no more than 300m each day. Walking higher during the day is fine as long as you descend to sleep. The commonly used phrase 'climb high – sleep low' allows for gentle acclimatisation.
* If campsites etc. are not conveniently placed every 300m, then for every 1000m of ascent, take a rest day. This will allow the body to catch up. Due to the individual nature of acclimatisation, some individuals will need extra days to adapt.

FIGURE 5.01 STARTING A TREK IN NEPAL, WITH LOTS MORE HEIGHT TO GAIN   Photo: Steve Long

- Incorporating a rest day every two to three days will help. Adopting a sensible ascent profile will ultimately reduce the risk of altitude-related illnesses and consequently increase the summit success rate.
- If planning a trek through a UK or overseas provider, discuss the altitude ascent profile with them. Discuss any room for adjusting the plan if the team or an individual is struggling to acclimatise.

5.4 Altitude illness

Many people going to altitude will complain of a headache, breathlessness and feeling slightly sick. These are some of the mild symptoms of AMS and often cause no more than discomfort to the individual. If the symptoms are ignored or deteriorate, with continued ascent, the individual may start to develop fluid in the brain, known as High altitude cerebral oedema (HACE) or fluid in the lungs, known as High altitude pulmonary oedema (HAPE). These conditions are serious and have a high mortality rate.

LAKE LOUISE SCORE CARD – FOR THE DIAGNOSIS OF AMS

A diagnosis of AMS is based on.

1 A rise in the altitude in the last 4 days
2 Presence of a headache
PLUS
3 Presence of at least one other symptom
4 A total score of 3 or more from the questionnaire below

Add together the individual scores for each symptom to get the **total score**.

AMS SCORECARD			TOTAL SCORE
Headache	None	0	
	Mild	1	
	Moderate	2	
	Severe/incapacitating	3	
Stomach/Guts	Good appetite	0	
	Poor appetite, nausea	1	
	Moderate nausea or vomiting	2	
	Severe/incapacitating	3	
Fatigue/Weakness	Not tired or weak	0	
	Mild fatigue/weakness	1	
	Moderate	2	
	Severe/incapacitating	3	
Dizziness/Light-headedness	None	0	
	Mild	1	
	Moderate	2	
	Severe/incapacitating	3	
Difficulty sleeping	As well as usual	0	
	Not as well as usual	1	
	Woke many times, poor night	2	
	Could not sleep at all	3	

TOTAL SCORE OF:	NOTE:
• 3 – 5 = mild AMS	• Do not ascend with symptoms of AMS
• 6 or more = severe AMS	• Descend if symptoms are not improving or getting worse
	• Descend if symptoms of HACE or HAPE develop

FIGURE 5.02   DIAGRAM OF AMS SCORECARD AND EXPLANATION

Altitude illness presents in the following three ways.

- *Acute mountain sickness (AMS):* common but not life threatening if dealt with correctly
- *High altitude pulmonary oedema (HAPE):* not common but life threatening.
- *High altitude cerebral oedema (HACE):* not common but life threatening.

5.5 Acute mountain sickness (AMS)

AMS varies from mild to severe and the main symptoms are due to fluid accumulating in and around the brain. Although breathlessness occurs instantly on arrival at altitude, AMS usually takes a few hours to develop. Typically, the symptoms appear within 12 hours of ascent. If no further ascent is made, AMS usually settles over one to three days as acclimatisation occurs. Further ascent may still cause AMS as acclimatisation to the new height has to take place all over again.

Common symptoms include the following.
- Headache – usually throbbing and often worse when bending or lying down

Plus one or more of the following symptoms.
- Fatigue and weakness
- Loss of appetite, nausea or vomiting
- Dizziness or light-headedness
- Poor sleep, disturbed sleep, frequent waking or periodic breathing (Cheyne Stokes)

FIGURE 5.03   SLEEPING AT ALTITUDE   Photo: Mal Creasey

- Become clumsy – stagger or fall over
- Act differently – unhelpful, violent, lazy
- Reduced level of consciousness
- Nausea or non-stop vomiting
- Blurred vision

A series of simple tests may help decide if the individual has HACE.

- Can they repeatedly touch a companion's finger and then their own nose (the companion should move their finger each time)?
- Can they walk heel to toe in a straight line?
- Can they stand upright with eyes closed and arms folded?
- Can they spell their name backwards or do simple arithmetic?

It is important to draw a comparison between an individuals' normal response to these tasks when you suspect HACE. Some individuals cannot balance on one leg even at sea level.

If the casualty is unable to perform or is having difficulty performing any of these tasks then HACE should be suspected and the casualty should descend immediately.

It is important to be honest about the feelings experienced at altitude and the use of a simple score card to monitor for any symptoms is an effective way to help make a diagnosis. Everyone will acclimatise at different rates but this score card can help make the decision whether to go up, have a rest day or go down.

5.6 High altitude cerebral oedema – HACE

High altitude cerebral oedema is caused by the accumulation of fluid in and around the brain. This swelling of the brain can kill very quickly if left untreated. HACE can develop very quickly sometimes without any other problems or it may follow AMS or HAPE.

Symptoms include the following.
- Severe headache – not relieved by ibuprofen, paracetamol or aspirin
- Loss of co-ordination (known as ataxia) – those affected may have difficulty with simple tasks such as tying their boots

5.7 High altitude pulmonary oedema – HAPE

HAPE is a serious condition caused by the build-up of fluid in the lungs that prevents the air spaces from opening up and filling with fresh air during each breath. HAPE may appear on its own without any preceding symptoms of AMS or it may develop at the same time as AMS or HACE. It can develop rapidly in one or two hours or over several days at altitudes above 2500 metres and commonly develops during or after the second night at a new height. Either way this is a serious condition and should be treated as soon as possible.

Symptoms include the following.
- Breathlessness at rest
- Extreme fatigue
- Coughing – a dry cough that develops into a wet cough
- Raised heart rate

- Lips, tongue and nails become blue due to lack of oxygen
- Crackling or gurgling sounds when the casualty breathes in deeply – put an ear close to their back, below the shoulder blades
- Froth and later blood in saliva
- Confusion and loss of consciousness

It may be easy to confuse the symptoms of HAPE with a chest infection or pneumonia. If in doubt, descend and treat for both.

5.8 Sleeping at high altitude

It is common, during the first few nights at altitude, to have disturbed sleep. Clients often complain of vivid dreams, feelings of suffocation and wake up feeling as though they have had little sleep. However, while the wind, the cold or room companions may all disturb the night's sleep, other more clinical reasons may cause poor sleep.

Deeper stages of sleep and rapid eye movement (REM) are reduced at altitude, therefore more of the night will be spent as light sleep and the sleep quality will not be as good as at sea level.

Periodic breathing (Cheyne Stokes breathing) is common at high altitude, occurring frequently

above 2800m and it may occur each time the sleeping height is raised. Symptoms of Cheyne Stokes are rapid breathing followed by periods when breathing briefly stops, often the person then gasps for breath sometimes causing them to wake up. Although this can be alarming and disturb sleep to both the individual and those around, it is not harmful and should improve with acclimatisation.

5.9 Treatment of altitude illness

For mild AMS, individuals should consider rest, rehydration and simple pain relief. Fluid loss at altitude is caused through increased breathing and sweating. Therefore aim to drink several litres of water throughout the day to offset this. Check urine output regularly to insure good hydration *(see **Chapter 4.10.3 Drinking** on page 77).*

Do not increase the sleeping height until all the symptoms are resolved. If there is no improvement, or the symptoms deteriorate – descend! Do not delay this decision; descending even 500 metres could help improve the condition. It is advisable to descend to a height where the individual last felt well, and to then allow extra time for acclimatisation before re-ascending.

In the event of suspecting HACE or HAPE then descend immediately.

- Stay with the casualty at all times – do not leave them unattended
- Sit them upright as this often makes breathing easier
- Keep them warm as the cold raises pulmonary artery pressure increasing the problems associated with HAPE
- Seek medical help
- Give oxygen via cylinder or hyperbaric bag if available
- For HACE give dexamethasone and acetazolamide
- For HAPE give nifedipine and acetazolamide
- If in doubt whether HAPE, HACE or a combination give all three drugs while preparing for the vital descent
- If descent is delayed consider prolonged use of a hyperbaric bag

FIGURE 5.04   TENT AT ALTITUDE
Photo: Outlook Expeditions

It is unlikely that a casualty suffering with HACE or HAPE will be able to walk; therefore a stretcher evacuation or piggy back will have to be arranged. While drugs are effective in the treatment of HACE and HAPE, these only buy time for essential descent and the use of additional oxygen.

5.10 Drugs at altitude

No trip to altitude should leave without certain medicines. Many will relieve symptoms making the trip more enjoyable; however some will save lives. Before departure seek the advice of a doctor about the suitability of any medication and confirm current practice with regard their administration. Many of these drugs are prescription only and could be regarded as suspect in certain countries. As mentioned previously always carry a letter from your doctor detailing your medicines to avoid legal problems.

Acetazolamide (trade name Diamox) is commonly used to reduce the effects of AMS, but should not be used in place of a sensible acclimatisation schedule. It can be useful if big height gains are unavoidable, such as arriving at La Paz (3880m) in Bolivia or if an individual is particularly susceptible to AMS. Acetazolamide increases

the breathing rate and speeds up the acclimatisation process.

Common side effects of using this drug include numbness and tingling in the fingers and toes, and taste alterations, especially for carbonated drinks. Some may also experience blurred vision but this usually disappears shortly after stopping the medication. Urine output is more frequent and as a result it becomes important to

FIGURE 5.05 BLURRED VISION AND NUMBNESS MAKE MOVEMENT MORE DIFFICULT Photo: Mike Rosser

FIGURE 5.06 HELICOPTER EVACUATION FROM NAMCHE Photo: Iain Peter

Dealing with altitude illnesses

Some people can be severly allergic to acetazolamide. Ask your clients to check with their doctor. As a leader, it might be worth considering investing in a stethoscope and pulsometer to add to your medical kit. With some training, these can help to identify some of the symptoms of AMS, HACE and HAPE.

FIGURE 5.07   A PAC BAG IN USE   Photo: Mal Creasey

drink more fluids than usual to prevent dehydration and headaches. It does not mask symptoms of AMS, and it is possible to suffer from AMS, HAPE and HACE while taking it.

Dexamethasone is a steroid drug used in the treatment of severe AMS and HACE. It reduces tissue swelling of the brain (oedema). The side effects include emotional problems after stopping the drug and depression and euphoria while taking it.

Nifedipine is commonly used in the treament of HAPE as it lowers the blood pressure in the pulmonary blood vessels thus decreasing fluid in the lungs. However, Nifedipine can lower the blood pressure enough to cause someone to fall or faint and therefore it should be used with caution.

Seeking advice of a doctor qualified in mountain medicine is important when dealing with these drugs.

5.11 Alternative medicines at altitude

Although untested and as yet not reviewed by medical researchers, there are many alternative drugs that can be taken to prevent or treat altitude related illnesses. Over time, garlic tablets thin blood, therefore are thought to be effective at improving circulation at altitude. Garlic soup is very often served for meals at higher altitudes. Commonly, Viagra (trade name) has been used in the treatment of HAPE but research continues to determine its effectiveness.

5.11.1 Hyperbaric bags

Portable hyperbaric bags are increasingly carried by high altitude trekking groups and are potentially available at most major base camps on popular trekking peaks around the world. The hyperbaric bag increases the air pressure to that found 2000m lower. It can provide a temporary improvement to a casualty's condition; however they are not a substitute for descent. An evacuation plan should already be in place and the relevant medication administered.

When using a hyperbaric bag the following considerations need to be made.

- The casualty will require constant monitoring and may require short breaks for examination and toilet purposes. Usually, the casualty remains in the bag for approximately one to two hours.
- A team of volunteers are necessary to continuously maintain pressure and airflow.
- The casualty will need to equalise pressure to their ears by pinching their nose and blowing.
- If the casualty needs oxygen, a bottle should be placed inside.
- A casualty will breathe more effectively (especially with HAPE) if the bag is angled so that the head is uphill. Fluid that collects around the lungs or brain tends to drain away more easily in a tilted position.
- If the casualty is losing consciousness, place them in the safe airway position within the bag and monitor their condition.
- Consider the environmental factors in the location of the bag. If in a cold environment the casualty will require warmth or they may need to be placed in the shade to avoid overheating.
- Casualties suffering from claustrophobia may be very anxious.
- Take an altimeter and pulse oximeter if available.

FIGURE 5.09   HIGH ALTITUDE TREKKING ON HORSEBACK, VACAS ROUTE ACONCAGUA   Photo: Helen Barnard

FIGURE 5.08   LOCAL YOUNG CHILDREN AT ALTITUDE
Photo: Outlook Expeditions

As a leader, it is important to be familiar in the use of hyperbaric bags.

5.12 Children at altitude

Trekking to remote and high places has become more popular with school and youth groups. The incidence of altitude related illness in children is the same as adults. However the diagnosis may prove more difficult in children too young to describe their symptoms. Any child who becomes unwell at altitude should be assumed to be having altitude illness until a clear alternative diagnosis is obvious. The treatment of children for AMS, HAPE and HACE remains the same as adults, however the quantities of drug administered vary according to the age of the child, and therefore it is important to seek advice from a qualified doctor.

 Leader's Information

The support team at altitude
When leading a trip to altitude the duty of care also extends to the support team (porters, cooks, etc.). At the start of the season, the support team, if they don't live at altitude, will need to acclimatise and are just as likely to suffer from altitude related illnesses as the clients. It is important that they communicate their symptoms and do not hide them for fear of loss of income. Differences in language should not be a barrier and a Lake Louise Score test should be translated into the local language. Keeping a daily diary on the symptoms your clients and support team are feeling will help in making a diagnosis of altitude related illnesses.

If travelling to altitude with a commercial operator, it is important to ask some key questions.

- What relevant experience and qualifications does the leader have?
- Do they have experience of leading expeditions to high altitude?
- Do they have knowledge of the use medicines, oxygen and maybe hyperbaric bags?
- What is the acclimatisation schedule for the trip?

FIGURE 5.10 TENGBOCHE SUPERMARKET   Photo: Mal Creasey

- What contingencies are there for clients with different acclimatisation rates?
- Are there additional days to allow for descent to a lower altitude?
- What are the plans in the event of someone falling ill with altitude sickness?

5.13 Additional problems at altitude

Trekking at altitude can place unusual stresses and strains on the body. Aside from altitude sickness there are a range of other issues to be aware of when travelling into this environment.

5.13.1 Peripheral oedema

Fluid retention in the face and hands is common at altitude and the condition usually subsides within a few days; however avoid wearing rings and tight clothing as this may lead to restrictive circulation in the extremities. It is not related to HAPE or HACE.

5.13.2 High altitude cough

The cold dry atmosphere at altitude may cause a sore throat and an irritating cough. Take plenty of throat lozenges that contain local anaesthetic on the expedition. Looking after the throat is important and some clients find breathing through a silk scarf or fabric facemask to warm up the air helpful. A cough can be a nuisance and severe coughing has been known to crack ribs.

5.13.3 Existing medical conditions

There is no evidence to suggest that clients suffering from asthma, diabetes or some other condition are any worse when travelling to altitude. The leader or companions should be aware of the symptoms of hypoglycaemia (low blood sugar level) and have access to glucose supplements. Diabetes may get worse at altitude. Many other pre-existing medical conditions can affect the body's ability to cope with altitude. Before travelling to altitude it is important to seek up-to-date medical advice from a doctor (preferably one qualified in mountain medicine). Find out about the risks involved and only travel if the condition is under control.

5.14 Dental problems

Before travelling to altitude visit the dentist. Rather than an extra visit schedule one to ensure you are up to date before you go. Cold air at altitude will cause pain to untreated broken fillings and cavities. Simple dental repair kits can provide a temporary solution until a more permanent option is available.

5.15 Food and nutrition at altitude

High altitude trekking, particularly in a cold environment, requires a lot of energy. Carbohydrates are the preferred energy source as fats are not tolerated well at altitude and require more oxygen for metabolism. Individuals at a high altitude should aim to eat approximately 400 grams of carbohydrate each day. Eating snack bars are a useful way to keep up the calorie count while moving and by carrying them inside jackets and clothing, they will remain soft and easy to eat.

It is important to drink regularly at altitude in order to avoid dehydration. Collecting water at high altitude may become increasingly difficult and time consuming. Running water may be impossible to find due to low temperatures, and melting snow and ice may be the only option. Above 5000 metres, an individual needs a minimum of 4 litres of fluid a day depending on their level of activity; therefore an organised system needs to be in place.

Once the water is melted, try to prevent it from refreezing. Keeping a warm water bottle inside the sleeping bag overnight (provided it doesn't leak) may initially provide warmth, and in the morning, provide enough water to make that all important warm drink. During the day, many people complain of water bottles freezing. By storing the water bottle next to the body, the heat generated through exercise will prevent this. If using a hydration bag and tube, blowing the water back into the bag helps prevent freezing of the tube.

 Leader's Information

Melting snow

If operating from a fixed camp, collect the snow and ice in a large black sealable dry bag and leave it in the tent during the day. The high temperatures encountered during the day will melt the snow and ice, saving time and fuel. If the camp location is moving daily, then the group needs to organise a rota where some are resting, others are collecting and melting snow and the stove is constantly on the go.

Spending time at high altitude requires both physical and mental preparation. Many people find it difficult to occupy themselves during rest days and complain of boredom particularly if a greater objective is planned, such as the ascent of a major peak. Within a group people may become frustrated at the slow walking pace, some members may feel anxious about the remoteness and consequences of potentially life threatening illnesses and some just find the lack of home comforts and living conditions difficult to deal with. It is important to be fully aware of what the trip involves in advance and to prepare yourself both physically and mentally. Anyone concerned about travelling to altitude is strongly advised to seek expert medical advice before embarking on the trek.

TREKKER STUDYING A MAP

Photo: www.pyb.co.uk

Proficiency with a map and compass has always been one of the cornerstones of any competent person venturing into the mountains.

FIGURE 6.01   WALKING SIGNPOSTS ABOVE ZINAL, SWITZERLAND   Photo: Bob Kinnaird

Navigating an appropriate route through a variety of terrain in challenging conditions requires a great deal of skill, knowledge and, above all, experience. Working in unfamiliar locations, with different maps and other navigational complications can stretch the most experienced navigator. There is no substitute for experience; however this can be difficult to develop when in a new country. Strategies based on principles used in more familiar places become even more important when trekking in unknown terrain.

Throughout the course of a trip the terrain may vary greatly; jungle to mountains to high desolate plateaus all of which will require a slightly different approach to successful navigation. On occasions the navigation may be very straightforward, especially when following popular trails or well marked routes. Many are established paths used by locals and communities that negate the need for fine detailed navigation and may not even necessitate the use of a map or compass.

However, having skills and equipment to fall back on is fundamental and very reassuring. Sometimes the most challenging navigational situations can catch us unawares, for instance the issues we may encounter when trying to find our way around the large towns or cities we encounter en route!

6.1 Map types

A good quality map is an essential tool for navigation. The quality of mapping throughout the British Isles is traditionally some of the best in the world. Sadly, this is not consistent with other countries and even for some parts of Europe the quality of mapping is more limited. This is often worse in developing countries where maps can be a combination of imagination along with some input from local inhabitants, rather than fact gained from a detailed survey.

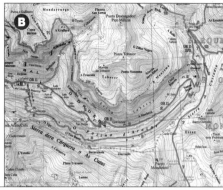

FIGURE 6.02   **A** AERIAL IMAGE OF ORDESA GORGE FROM GOOGLE EARTH   **B** MAP OF ORDESA GORGE

Using maps with limited information requires a flexible approach. Sourcing maps well before a trip is therefore important to allow time to become familiar with the scale, symbols and the amount of information available. This is an obvious necessity when planning and can prevent surprises when faced with an odd looking map for the first time in-country. Maps will vary greatly in the scales and symbols they use and the grid system they adopt. Taking an existing map and adding notes from discussions with locals is a good idea.

6.2 Procuring maps

Sourcing foreign maps can present issues and generally the further afield the destination the longer the period required for obtaining any relevant maps and guides. Various agencies can supply maps for most regions across the globe and purchase can often be made over the internet; however the maps gained are not always the best available or fit for purpose. When viewing a map search for the "Print Note" or "Compilation Note" in the map margin. Most maps will show when the map was compiled, and the age of the information used to create it when it was printed. Do not be misled by a print date of 2010 when in fact the map was compiled in 1938.

For remote countries, military maps by their nature offer a good deal of information. However procurement is often only the first problem. Many countries still regard their maps as official state secrets: being caught with one in your possession could land you in trouble. Some states

are more liberal with this information and with a little research it may be possible to obtain a more detailed map for the area you are visiting. Embassies or consulates can often help with advice regarding these matters. Other sources are trekking companies and individuals who visit areas on a regular basis As well as providing a wealth of useful information they may be able to assist with details on mapping for the area.

Often when operating near borders it may be possible to obtain maps from two different countries for the same area of land (Spain, France, Alps, etc.). This can provide more information and on occasions a more accurate map better suited for purpose.

6.3 Satellite imagery

Satellite imagery can also be used to complement maps acquired for an expedition. The internet provides a great source for this information; however the different types of projections can be overwhelming so take time to research the most appropriate material. It may be worth planning to research and print satellite imagery in colour before leaving home.

6.4 Aerial photography

Another useful augmentation to any mapping is aerial photography. As with satellite imagery there are many sources for aerial photography. Obtaining images over any western European country will not prove too difficult, but the further away the destination the harder this will become – this is mainly the result of security restrictions. It is worth remembering that aerial images are nearly always distorted and do not necessarily represent the ground perfectly. Internet sites such as Google Earth can now provide us with this type of information in an instant. And while this may not always be up to date it can provide a useful complement to an existing map.

Before departure, laminate any maps or images to preserve them through the various conditions they may be subjected to. This will make it easier to annotate them as you travel, allowing adjustments to be made as inaccuracies are discovered.

6.5 Symbols

Throughout the British Isles Ordnance Survey use symbols known as conventional signs to represent features on the ground. The signs provide an extraordinary level of information and attached to every map a key provides a way of deciphering their meaning. This is not always the case with foreign maps; some may not even have a complete key showing the meaning of all the signs and symbols used (in some cases a separate document may have to be purchased). Although common sense may help in deciding the meaning of a particular symbol, it may only be possible once the feature has been seen on the ground. This may require the user to make a key as they are travelling.

6.6 Contour interpretation

It is generally accepted that the best way to represent a three-dimensional landscape in two dimensions is to use contour lines. The use of contour lines to show shape and relief on maps from other countries can vary dramatically. Some maps may well have areas that show contour lines and other areas where the lines are absent due to a lack of accurate information.

If the shape of land is to be fully understood the users needs to make themselves familiar with both the scale of the map and the contour interval. This can make an enormous difference for two maps with the same horizontal scale yet different contour intervals. Contours spaced one millimetre apart may represent a twenty-degree slope on one map, but a forty-degree slope on another. Most maps give an indication of this interval either on the map, in the key, or on the grid margin.

In the absence of accurate contour inform-ation or a low contour interval shading and or colour is sometimes used to help define relief for an area. These maps can appear very different and in some cases it adds to the level of detail making them appear almost three dimensional. In other examples it can confuse and greatly hinder the ability to relate ground to map and vice versa.

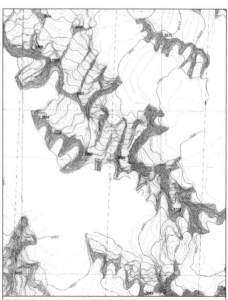

FIGURE 6.04   MAP SECTION SHOWING ABSENCE OF INFORMATION, GREENLAND

FIGURE 6.03   KEY TAKEN FROM FOREIGN MAP

6.7 Compasses

For centuries the magnetic compass has been a fundamental tool in the armoury of any navigator. Beyond giving direction, most modern compasses are useful for a variety of other tasks, in particular measuring distances from the map (those that have rulers or map scales known as romers). To work properly, the compass needle must be free to rotate and align with the earth's magnetic field. Don't store your telephone or other magnetic or electronic devices near your compass. Because the magnetic field varies around the world a typical compass will only function without problems within a set range of longitudes. For example, the difference between compasses designed to work in the northern and southern hemispheres is simply the location of the "balance", a weight placed on the needle to ensure it remains in a horizontal plane and hence is free to rotate. Various manufacturers have innovated a solution to this problem and as a result have produced a 'global compass' suitable for use throughout the world.

6.8 Magnetic declination

Magnetic declination is the angle between magnetic north (the direction the north end of a compass needle points) and true north. Magnetic declination varies both from place to place, and with the passage of time. For example, as a traveller moves east across North America, the declination varies from 17 degrees east in Vancouver (western seaboard) to 19 degrees west in Maine (eastern seaboard), meaning a compass adjusted at the beginning of the journey would have a true north error of 36 degrees if not adjusted for the changing declination.

The magnetic declination in a given area will change slowly over time, possibly as much as 2–25 degrees every hundred years or so, depending upon how far from the magnetic poles it is. Complex fluid motion in the outer core of the earth (the molten metallic region that lies from 2800 to 5000km below the earth's surface) causes

FIGURE 6.05   A WORLD COMPASS IN ACTION
Photo: Carlo Forte

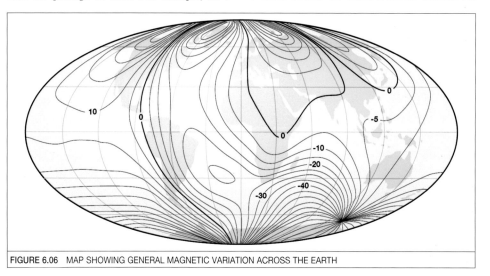

FIGURE 6.06   MAP SHOWING GENERAL MAGNETIC VARIATION ACROSS THE EARTH

the magnetic field to change slowly with time. This change is known as secular variation. Because of secular variation, declination values shown on old maps need to be updated if they are to be used without large errors. Unfortunately, the annual change corrections given on most maps cannot be applied reliably since the secular variation also changes unpredictably with time. Therefore if time is to be spent using bearings en route, the magnetic declination for the region will need to be investigated. This information can be found using various websites or alternatively most GPS units can be setup to show magnetic variation at its location.

6.9 Using guide books

Many travellers' guides (Lonely Planet, Footprint, etc.) and guidebooks provide useful information for those venturing into the wilderness. They also make a good companion when trying to navigate around a large town or city. In these situations it is worth extracting the most useful information rather than using the whole book, as this is less likely to attract attention. Popular routes and itineraries are often covered by a range of literature that range from indepth guidebooks to personal accounts of individual trips.

Specific guidebooks to wilderness areas often provide information about routes, accommodation, weather, hazards and organising

logistics. While this is extremely useful it is worth remembering things change over time hence the reason for obtaining information from a variety of sources. All this information can be put to good use while planning but can also assist when in-country. However, to avoid shipping a library out to a destination it is worth compiling a fact file for the area and the trip. This can be a condensed version of all the information gained from research.

6.10 Finding North on an unmarked map

Most maps produced follow the same convention of being orientated to North (grid north). Many will show a grid devised from a datum line, usually grid north. This is an artificial concept designed for communicating positions; it is the northerly direction of the North-South grid lines on a map. Maps will often show in the margins how the grid is constructed and the relationship between the three north poles. This information is used when determining the magnetic variation and for orientating the map.

Knowing where North on the map lies allows the user to set the map with ease. The norm is for this to be the top, that is the map reads like a book; top is North, bottom is South, left is West and right is East. Having said this some maps

FIGURE 6.07   TREKKER REFERRING TO A GUIDEBOOK   Photo: www.pyb.co.uk

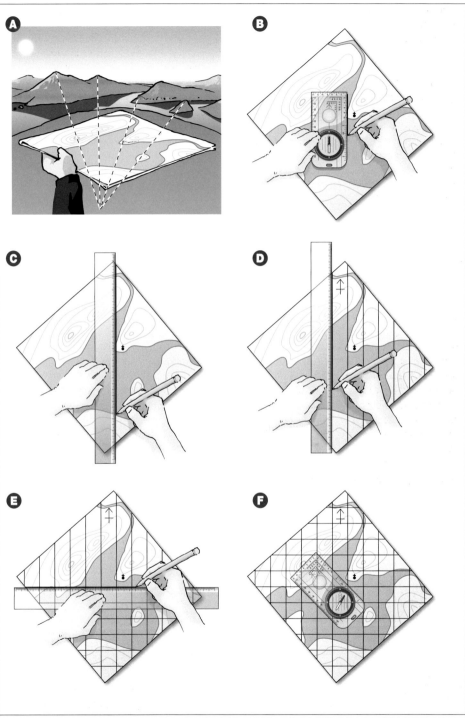

FIGURE 6.08 DRAWING A GRID ON A MAP THAT HAS NO GRID LINES: **A** ORIENTATE THE MAP USING IDENTIFIABLE FEATURES. **B** SET COMPASS TO MAGNETIC NORTH AND USE EDGE TO START DATUM LINE. **C** USE A RULER TO DRAW A DATUM LINE. **D** DRAW PARALLEL LINES EQUAL DISTANCE FROM DATUM. **E** DRAW LINES AT 90° TO DATUM TO CREATE A GRID OF SQUARES. **F** MAP CAN NOW BE USED TO TAKE BEARINGS.

may not follow this convention. While a map can be used without these features it makes sense to determine them beforehand, especially when operating in complex terrain or when having to take bearings. The accuracy of any bearing is based on how well it is taken from a map and this can only be achieved with an accurate grid in place. If a grid is not shown, but there is reference information shown around the margins of the map, then it may be possible to link corresponding co-ordinates with straight lines. This will create a series of northings and eastings. If no information is shown it becomes a much more laborious process to establish a useful grid.

6.11 Establishing a grid

A distinctive feature of British maps is the grid structure of lines superimposed over the whole country. These grid lines form the basis of a numerical system, which allows any point to have its own unique reference. To establish an effective grid there needs to be a series of identifiable features shown on both the map and the ground. This will allow the map to be set using these ground features. Once orientated a compass set to grid north can be laid onto the

map (check magnetic declination and add or subtract the appropriate amount). This will define a grid north on the map and allow a line to be marked. This can then be used as a datum from which other lines can be marked at equal spacing. A complete grid can be produced from this by adding lines set at 90° to the original datum. Finally by adding in co-ordinates a reference system for any location can be created. This may seem crude but it may well be of great assistance to anyone monitoring progress from a base or co-ordinating a rescue.

6.12 Latitude and longitude

There are two common co-ordinate systems used on maps across the world: latitude and longitude, and UTM (Universal Transverse Mercator). Developed and implemented by mariners and explorers in the Middle Ages to help guide them across the oceans, latitude and longitude is the oldest of these systems. It divides the earth into lines of latitude, which indicate how far north or south of the equator you are, and lines of longitude, which indicate how east or west you are of the prime meridian.

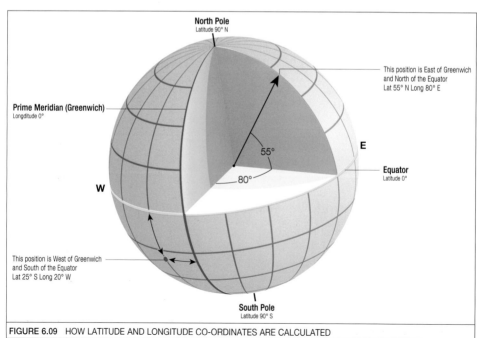

FIGURE 6.09   HOW LATITUDE AND LONGITUDE CO-ORDINATES ARE CALCULATED

The combination of lines of longitude (meridians) and lines of latitude (parallels) establishes a grid by which exact positions can be determined. For example, a point described as 40° N, 30° W is located 40° of arc north of the equator and 30° of arc west of the Greenwich meridian.

To precisely locate points on the earth's surface, degrees of longitude and latitude are divided into minutes (') and seconds ("), which relate to the geometry of a circle as opposed to time. There are 60 minutes in each degree with each minute being divided into 60 seconds. Seconds can be further divided into tenths, hundredths, or even thousandths.

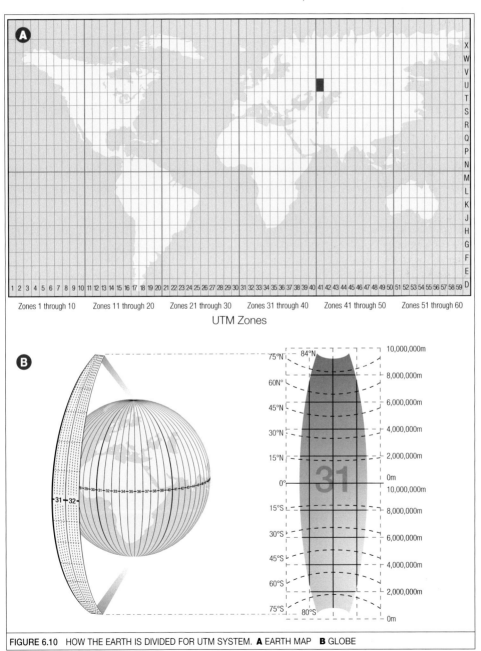

FIGURE 6.10   HOW THE EARTH IS DIVIDED FOR UTM SYSTEM. **A** EARTH MAP   **B** GLOBE

- 1° of Latitude is 111.12km (69 miles)
- 1' is one nautical mile (1.85km or 1.15miles)
- 1" is approximately 100 feet (30 metres)

Because lines of longitude converge at the poles the distances between them decreases as they move further from the equator.

- 1° of Longitude is 111.12km (69 miles) only at the equator, at 45° N or S it is only 78km (49 miles).
- 1' is only one nautical mile (1.85km or 1.15 miles) at the equator.

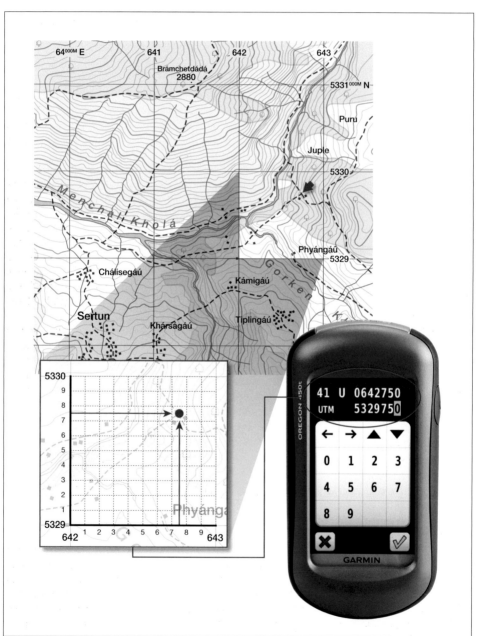

FIGURE 6.11 TAKING A UTM REFERENCE FOR USE WITH A GPS UNIT. NOTE HOW THE MAP REFERENCE 41U MATCHES THE HIGHLIGHTED BOX IN **FIGURE 6.10A** AND PREFIXES THE REFERENCE NUMBER

There are three ways of expressing longitude and latitude for any given location.

1 Hemisphere degrees minutes and seconds
   hddd°.mm'.ss.s".
2 Hemisphere degrees and decimal minutes
   hddd°.mm.mmm'.
3 Hemisphere decimal degrees
   hddd.ddddd°.

YES TOR ON DARTMOOR = SX 581 902	
N 50° 41' 36.3" W 4° 0' 37.6"	hddd°.mm'.ss.s"
N 50° 41.6' W 4° 0.616'	hddd°.mm.mmm'
N 50.69333 W 4.01027	hddd.ddddd°

FIGURE 6.12 EXAMPLE OF THE THREE WAYS OF EXPRESSING LONGITUDE AND LATITUDE

The most commonly used method is *degrees and decimal minute's* ddd°.mm.mmm'

Most maps show latitude and longitude scales running along their edges. Their ease of use will depend on how the map has been printed. On some maps even though the scales are shown in the margins there is no grid overlaying the map making it difficult to pinpoint the co-ordinates of a location (see section on establishing a grid).

It is possible to measure co-ordinates with your eyes; however the easiest and most accurate method involves using a specifically calibrated minute/second ruler.

6.13 Universal Transverse Mercator

The Universal Transverse Mercator system is probably the most commonly used map projection. It was adopted by the US Army in 1947 for designating co-ordinates on large scale military maps and has since been developed to set a universal worldwide system for mapping. Still used by the US military and NATO it can also be found on many foreign maps and is often shown alongside the longitude and latitude grid system.

The UTM system divides the earth into 60 zones each 6 degrees of longitude wide. These zones extend from a latitude of 80° south to 84° north. Neither of the poles are included in the

UTM system; instead a separate grid known as Universal Polar Stereographic (UPS) is used.

UTM zones are numbered 1 to 60, starting at the International Date Line, longitude 180°, and proceeding east *(see Figure 6.10A on page 77)*.

Each zone is divided into horizontal bands, designated by a letter. The letters O and I are skipped to avoid confusion with the numbers one and zero. A square grid is superimposed and aligned so that grid lines are parallel to the centre of the zone, called the central meridian.

The UTM system is designed so that you read horizontal distances eastward and vertical distances northward from reference lines. This is the same as using the Ordnance Survey grid reference system. Not surprisingly these are referred to as the 'easting', and a distance in metres to the north, referred to as the 'northing'.

As with the Ordnance Survey system it is possible to use both sets of co-ordinates to create a reference number unique to a particular location on the map. A complete UTM reference includes the UTM zone number and band letter followed firstly by the 'easting' and then by the 'northing'.

Eastings are made up of 6 digits as opposed to northings which are made up of 7. The convention is to add a 0 at the start of the eastings. This is particularly important when entering this information into a GPS.

Some UTM northing values are valid for both the northern and southern hemisphere. In order to avoid confusion the full co-ordinate needs to specify if the location is north or south of the equator. This is done by including the letter for the latitude band *(see Figure 6.11)*.

6.14 Strategies (gathering clues, breaking routes into sections)

Many of the popular trekking destinations are well catered for with both maps and a good network of paths, particularly on the more established routes. In places signage and waymarking also help to guide the way. Switzerland is an example of where this system is used extensively not just to guide walkers but also to inform them of the nature of the terrain. Different colour

FIGURE 6.13   CLEAR SIGNAGE OR WAYMARKING
ABROAD   Photo: www.pyb.co.uk

FIGURE 6.14   SUBTLE WAYMARKING (PAINT ON
ROCKS)   Photo: www.pyb.co.uk

FIGURE 6.15   WAYMARKED BOULDER
                          Photo: www.pyb.co.uk

coding on signs and waymarks allows people to plan a journey appropriate to their ability, and because this is a system adopted throughout the country, the maps also show this information. Various countries, national parks and other organisations adopt similar systems to help inform and guide.

Following paths and signs may seem straightforward but it is important to draw on our basic navigation skills in these situations to avoid becoming lost and wasting time. In good conditions navigation along these features consists mainly of keeping track of the direction and the distance travelled. Along the way a variety of features are likely to be passed at intervals allowing the navigator to re-affirm their position. These tick features can be likened to the stations passed on a train journey: As long as the train

remains on the tracks then stations will be passed in the right order.

In poor conditions, although still straightforward, more effort should be made to take note of these features and possibly the distances in between, plus the direction travelled. This is particularly useful when arriving at decision points (junctions, etc.) and having to relocate before deciding the route to the next destination. Signage can obviously provide great assistance at these points, but it is always worth a quick check of the map to confirm the correct location. Estimated times on signage is just that, an estimate. It is worth gauging a group's progress against the estimation on the signage. Paths change over seasons, especially if terrain is subject to movement (land slips, etc.). Signage may or may not, depending on how recently any changes occurred. The map may also give no indication of a change. Either way this can lead to confusion, so time taken to confirm position and the direction to next destination could be time saved later.

Many features can be used as handrails. These may be very easy to follow, or require great skill particularly in poor visibility. Suitable linear features include footpaths, fences, walls, stream and rivers. Landforms are of particular note, especially in the greater ranges where it is possible to follow a large valley or river for a

FIGURE 6.16   RELATING THE MAP TO THE GROUND IN
TRIGLAV NATIONAL PARK   Photo: www.pyb.co.uk

FIGURE 6.17   USING GPS INFORMATION TO HELP
CONFIRM POSITION   Photo: www.pyb.co.uk

number of days. While this may seem straight-forward being able to identify your position within the valley could still be important in determining the distance travelled and the distance left to travel.

6.15 Timings/speeds/altitude

Timing can be used in a number of ways. As a planning tool it can give an indication of how much is feasible in a given time or how long a trip may take if a steady average pace is maintained. With practice it can be used to accurately time short distances to help reach destinations in difficult conditions. Accuracy can vary greatly depending on a numbers of factors, all of which should be considered in any calculations. Distance, conditions underfoot, weather, fitness can all influence speed. Another factor that may need to be considered is the total length of journey given that fatigue over a period will reduce speed. Altitude and acclimatisation will also need to be considered as speed is influenced greatly by these factors. It is important to factor these variables into any calculations at the planning stage, and use them to monitor progress while en route. Route cards and aide memoirs can be produced before the trip to assist with this process.

6.16 Use of Global Positioning System (GPS)

Designed originally for military defence use, Global Positioning System technology has become increasingly sophisticated and accessible. The system has been designed to work pretty much anywhere on the planet. However, it is worth remembering that since a GPS unit may lose track of satellites, run out of power, or break, it should not be relied on solely for navigation particularly when used on extended expeditions. Used in combination with other navigational skills it can be a very powerful tool, especially in featureless terrain or where mapping information is limited. Therefore consider a GPS unit as a tool and always carry a compass and a map.

One of the best functions a GPS unit can perform is the ability to provide accurate location information. Using good signals from four well placed satellites it can provide an accurate 3D fix, such as location and altitude. If signals from only three satellites are being used the unit may provide a 2D fix; however the location given may be inaccurate and the unit will compensate for the missing satellite by estimating the elevation. Once locked onto satellites the GPS unit will display a continuously updated position *(see Figure 6.18).*

FIGURE 6.18 THE SATELLITE PAGE GIVES A REPRE-
SENTATION OF SATELLITE GEOMETRY. THE BAR
GRAPHS SHOW SATELLITES BEING LISTENED TO AND
THE STRENGTH OF THE SIGNALS BEING RECEIVED.
AN ESTIMATED POSITION ERROR (EPE) IS GIVEN TO
INDICATE THE ACCCURACY OF THE POSITION SHOWN.
IN THIS EXAMPLE, IT SUGGESTS ± 5 METRES

FIGURE 6.19 SCREEN SHOT OF A MAPPING GPS
DISPLAYING FOREIGN MAP

Beyond just giving a location, GPS units can provide the operator with additional information that can be used to navigate effectively. The user can program waypoints (locations) that can then be navigated to or saved in a memory for use later. When navigating to a location the unit can be set up to show a variety of information that can assist with navigation such as estimated time of arrival (ETA), distance to destination, speed over terrain and direction. This information can also be used to cross-reference and help confirm calculations and decisions made from the map. Many units are sold with the option of a barometric altimeter; used in the same way as any other digital altimeter it will show ascent and descent plus trends in pressure for weather prediction (see **Use of altimeters** page 84).

Many GPS units now include very simple worldwide base maps as standard. More detailed mapping can be sought although at present this is not worldwide. Depending on the manufacturer and the country being visited it may or may not be possible to purchase compatible digital maps. If the intention were to use GPS some research before hand as to the availability of software for the unit would be necessary (see Figure 6.19).

GPS manufacturers offer pre-set options for various position formats and map datums commonly used around the world. Where a country has no common system or map datum options the unit can always be set to latitude/longitude. At the very least this will give a location that can be used for future reference or given to the rescue services if help is required.

On arrival in-country and prior to the start of any trip there are some steps that should be taken to ensure the GPS unit is correctly set up for use. The first and most important consid-

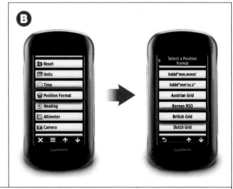

FIGURE 6.20 **A** SETUP OF TRIP COMPUTER PAGE TO SHOW RELEVANT DATA **B** SETTING POSITION FORMAT TO
CORRESPOND WITH MAP BEING USED

FIGURE 6.21 TREKKER COMBINING MAP AND GPS INFORMATION Photo: www.pyb.co.uk

eration is to make sure the GPS unit settings (position formats and map datums) reflect that of the maps being used. For example to set up a GPS unit for use in the UK the position format will need to be set to British grid. Most units will then automatically select the corresponding map datum *(see Figure 6.20)*.

All measurement units should be set to the same as those of the map. This will make cross-referencing of information between the unit and the map much easier.

Prior to starting any journey it is worth thinking about how you intend to use GPS. If there is a need for its use on a regular basis over a long period of time there will be issues with the amount of power available. Using the functions regularly places increased demands on battery power. The same can also be said for using them in cold conditions. Carrying large quantities of batteries to cope with a long expedition may not be practical. Disposable lithium batteries are much lighter than standard batteries; they last longer and perform better in a wider variety of conditions. Re-chargeable batteries may not last as long in use but the big advantage is the reduction in the quantity required and with modern technology lightweight solar rechargers are available negating the need to always have to find a power source. For best performance with GPS units it is important to use re-chargeables with a rating greater than 2000mh.

If the intention is to log a number of waypoints en-route and or record the route in detail for

FIGURE 6.22 MOUNTING AND CARRYING OF GPS ON SHOULDER STRAP OF RUCKSACK Photo: Carlo Forte

future reference, demands will be placed on the amount of information that can be stored within the unit's memory. Over a prolonged period of time this may exceed the unit's memory capacity. Therefore before embarking on any long journey try to free up as much memory space as possible. Any unnecessary information such as waypoints, tracks or routes from other trips should be saved elsewhere and deleted from the memory. Many manufacturers provide software to assist with the storage of this information using a PC, although there is also a wealth of freeware and shareware available from other sources. Some units have the option of increasing their memory capacity with small flash cards. If the expedition is long and requires a lot of data to be stored having spare cards to download this information onto will prevent the unit from reaching its capacity and allow for a complete record of the trip.

Where the unit is carried or mounted if it is to record any route information accurately requires some consideration. Buried in a rucksack and it will struggle to detect signals from satellites meaning it will loose reception and be unable to record information. Good examples of places to carry a GPS unit so as to get best reception while travelling include in the top pocket or on the shoulder strap of a rucksack *(see Figure 6.22)*. Many units use a patch (flat) antenna which requires the receiver to be held or mounted level for best results.

GPS can be a very powerful tool; however there are potential issues with its use in the field. A unit will work best when it has full unobscured view of the sky. In featureless terrain, plateaus, deserts (ice caps) this can be easily achieved and provide a great source of information and comfort when determining position. In steep-sided valleys, jungle/wooded terrain or close to large cliffs or buildings the view of the sky may be obscured and therefore the unit may struggle to find and utilise the necessary satellite information required for accuracy. This proves further the need for good map and compass skills to combine with other information in these situations *(see Figure 6.21)*.

It is important to fully understand the functions of the GPS unit being used. Time spent familiarising oneself with the required settings and workings of the unit will be time saved later. It will also serve to help understand the information given more clearly.

6.17 Use of altimeters

An altimeter is great lightweight addition to your equipment and when used properly more than justifies its carriage.

Unlike a GPS unit, an altimeter does not depend on external systems for accuracy and can work in virtually any conditions. Analogue altimeters need no batteries so are almost impervious to cold and they are incredibly reliable. Digital altimeters are typically very flexible supporting a range of additional features. Some GPS units come equipped with a built in barometric altimeter which can still be used even when the unit is unable to detect signals from satellites.

FIGURE 6.23 **A** DIGITAL AND **B** ANALOGUE ALTIMETERS

The heart of an altimeter is an aneroid box: a sealed capsule that contracts or expands as air pressure varies. Changes in air pressure are displayed or converted to altitude readings. Since air pressure does not change directly in proportion to height, it is therefore important to combine the use of an altimeter with an accurate map and to reset the reference altitude regularly.

Most altimeters offer readings in two formats: absolute altitude and relative altitude. Absolute altitude is the height above (or below) sea level; relative altitude is the height above (or below) a reference point. The absolute reading is particularly useful when locating a position on a map using the contour lines or determining how much further to go to a given landmark. Relative altitude measurement is most useful for targeting an altitude gain to avoid climbing too high or on a descent to avoid overshooting and having to climb back up. Night and poor visibility navigation can be significantly enhanced with the extra information provided by an altimeter.

Altimeters measure atmospheric pressure and convert this to an altitude reading. So by definition an altimeter is also a barometer and therefore capable of helping make weather observations. This can be very useful in the absence of good weather information. If your altitude remains constant for any period of time, such as overnight camp, but the altimeter reading continues to climb then atmospheric pressure is falling and could indicate deterioration in the current weather. Generally, falling pressure of 2mbar or more per hour indicates deterioration in the weather. The reverse is also true – if your a camp or key navigational feature or as a warning on the descent to avoid a hazard noticed during the climb up. The generally accepted wisdom of 'aiming-off' with an altimeter is to aim low when ascending and aim high when descending which in both cases avoids over-shooting the target and having to backtrack.

The biggest advantage they offer is the potential for greater accuracy when navigating in sloped terrain. Contouring can be difficult, particularly in poor visibility; the tendency to walk slightly down/uphill in these situations can be removed by simply monitoring for any indicated change in altitude.

6.18 Using in-country support

Many people use in-country support to help get around for all or part of a trip. As well as providing links with local facilities and support with language issues they may also provide a guiding service for your intended itinerary. While this may take the pressure off having to make navigational decisions on a regular basis it is important that you spend time following the route closely and involve yourself as far as possible in the decision making. In-country support may not have the same level of expertise as a UK leader or the same understanding of the duty of care of a leader operating to the UK standards. It is therefore prudent for a leader to know where they are and what rescue, shelter and shortcut options are available. Local guides can range from being highly competent to a lot less! This will allow monitoring of the route and warning of any potential mistakes sooner rather than later.

While the thought of having to navigate in unfamiliar surroundings with unreliable information may seem difficult, success can be made through learning how to apply existing skills. The basic skills gained from experience of navigating in a variety of conditions in more familiar terrain will give confidence when confronted with more challenging situations.

FIGURE 6.24 USING IN-COUNTRY SUPPORT TO HELP WITH ROUTE FINDING   Photo: Mal Creasey

height remains constant but the altitude reading falls it indicates an increase in atmospheric pressure and with that an improvement in weather conditions. Digital altimeters often provide pressure tendency displays that show the trend over a period of time. Failing this if a note of the altitude is made on arrival at a location (such as campsite) and then noted again on departure (plus possibly at regular intervals in between) if there is any change, rise or fall in altitude it will give an indication of the pressure trend.

The accuracy of altimeters will depend on three main factors.

- The altitude change since the last calibration.
- The length of time since the last calibration.
- The atmospheric pressure change due to changing weather and/or location.

As with GPS the altimeter should be consid-ered an additional tool to assist with navigation. Many altimeters have the facility to set upper and lower limit alarms providing an indication that you have arrived at a predetermined altitude. This is useful on ascent to prevent over-ascending and suffering from altitude sickness or to locate

Trekking hazards

TREKKING IN THE SPECTACULARLY EXPOSED FAYA DE LAS FLORES, ORDESA

Photo: Nigel Williams

All trekking journeys and adventures involve a certain amount of risk, that's often the reason people are involved. They enjoy the challenge and the uncertainty of outcome, and often embrace the challenge of assessing risks and making decisions on the move.

7

FIGURE 7.01 CAREFULLY NEGOTIATING A STEEP SECTION OF TERRAIN

Photo: www.pyb.co.uk

Before travelling to particular areas it makes sense to carry out some research. This can help identify hazards which might be unique to that environment, and help develop an awareness of them before arrival. Having gained information about these hazards it is then possible to decide how best to manage them beforehand.

• Identify the hazards	**Recognise Hazards**
• Decide who could be harmed by them and how	
• How likely is it to go wrong?	**Assess risk**
• Is the level of risk acceptable? (Whose decision is this?)	**Value judgement**
• Is there a need for further action?	**Action/control measures**
• Monitor and re-evaluate this process	**Review**

7.1 Risk management

Much of our day to day management of risk occurs subconsciously, so in many settings it can be useful to have a formal system for the process. This is especially true if we have limited experience of the activity and/or the environment. Prior planning allows people to make informed decisions about possible risks and at the same time consider their own/the group's capabilities, in order to maximise their potential. The following sequence needs to be examined for this to be successful:

7.2 Risk assessment

Assessment of risk is required at various stages of a trip in order to make an informed judgement about the balance of human, environmental and timing factors. Hazards are inherent in all mountain walks and recognising them is a fundamental part of any risk assessment process. However hazards will always exist and only become a risk when we choose to interact with them. For this reason it is important to consider the nature of this interaction before making any judgements.

FIGURE 7.02 DO YOU FEEL LUCKY? Photo: Simon Hale

A simple approach to this is to consider the following:

- **Who** is going?

  The number of people on the trip is an important consideration. Their experience should match the aims and objectives. Many factors can make things more challenging; difficult group dynamics, financial pressures, last minute changes, large or small groups.

- **Where** are you going?

  Information about the location, the terrain and the specific type of hazards are often available from guide books, maps, tourist offices and the internet. Talking to people who have previously visited the area can also provide some valuable information. Remoteness, rescue and seriousness of location all require careful consideration.

- **When** are you going?

  Some trekking venues have definite seasons outside which conditions are often inappropriate. Operating trips outside the seasonal norms could increase the hazard due to a number of factors; weather conditions, lack of local support and facilities, for example tea houses, medical centres and in some cases rescue support.

- **Why** are you going?

  Reasons for going on trips are very varied, from once in a life-time trips, to the annual holiday, to people who sign up for charity treks. What motivates the group and individual is an important factor when considering and managing risk. People will have different views on the levels of risk they are prepared to deal with. Good communication between members at the planning stage will help to reach a consensus.

- **Weather**

  The weather can make or sometimes break a trip and different conditions can greatly increase the level of hazard experienced. Unseasonal or extreme weather may mean changes have to be made to planned trekking routes. Constant evaluation of conditions and how these are affecting the environment is paramount *(see **Chapter 8 Weather** on page 111)*.

7.2.1 Site specific hazards

Experience allows us to make judgement about the inherent hazards beforehand; loose rock, rivers and weather. However despite all the planning there may be specific hazards that exist which are difficult to anticipate and may only become apparent when confronted. Therefore it is necessary to adopt a flexible and more dynamic approach to assessment and management of these situations to ensure the hazards are dealt with appropriately.

Guidebooks and the internet can provide vital information about intended areas to visit, and often help in the planning and logistics. Talking to people who have trekked in the area is also an invaluable source of up-to-date information. Some of the major trekking organisations are useful contacts when trying to find out about a particular area, and the hazards present. All this information can be used to help manage risk and plan effectively for journeys in unfamiliar environments. From a planning perspective, information is power, and as the old saying states 'time spent in reconnaissance is seldom wasted.'

⊕ Leader's Information

Involving the group in risk management

An important part of a leader's work is to make sure the group understand the level of risk involved in any activity they chose to participate in. The leader should aim to create an environment in which group members are able to contribute to any discussion or decisions with regards risk. Risk management and avoidance of high risk are important during any journey and once informed of the hazards and associated risks participants should have the option to decide what level of risk they are prepared to accept. The leader's role is to understand the group and their aims and aspirations, and match these appropriately to the journey. When confronted with unforeseen situations the leader will need to discuss any decisions with the group and allow them to voice any opinions or concerns they may have.

Photo: www.pyb.co.uk

7.3 Recognising the hazards

Hazards are situations that pose a risk to life, health or the environment (a risk is the potential that a chosen action or activity will result in an undesirable outcome).

Hazards can be categorised into three interlinked components.

- Human
- Environmental
- Timing

7.3.1 Human

Human error is often a key factor in many incidents in the hills and generally stems from inadequate communication or lack of experience and associated poor judgement. When travelling as a team, dialogue with all those involved at every stage is important in order to inform about the nature of any risks and the plans used to manage them. The following list outlines some of the points to discuss to raise individuals' awareness and help to involve them with this process.
- Aims and objectives of the trip
- Anticipated terrain and weather

- Inherent and specific hazards and control measures
- Cultures and customs of the destination
- Clothing and equipment
- Food and drink
- Medical conditions and illness
- Transport
- Costs
- Individual and collective responsibilities
- Behaviour
- Contact meeting places
- Contingency plans

With good communication among group members many potential risks can be reduced. Encouraging ongoing dialogue will help to involve everyone in the process, thus helping to build a strong team unit.

Risk with regard to the human factor can manifest itself in a number of other ways; from illness contracted while on the trip; to injury due to a small slip.

7.3.2 Environmental

Aside from the generic hazards found in all mountain regions the sheer scale of many of the mountains in Europe and the Greater Ranges can

FIGURE 7.03 HAZARDOUS RIVER CROSSING IN
INDONESIA   Photo: Mal Creasey

present a risk. The psychological and physical effects of some treks may need careful consideration and management.

The scale of many mountains can also present difficulties associated with assessing risks from above. By their nature mountains are places that are less predictable and very dynamic. This makes risk assessment more challenging and often a bigger margin for error needs to be built in to the process.

FIGURE 7.04 A TREK IN THE BIG MOUNTAINS, ANNAPURNA SANCTUARY, NEPAL   Photo: Steve Long

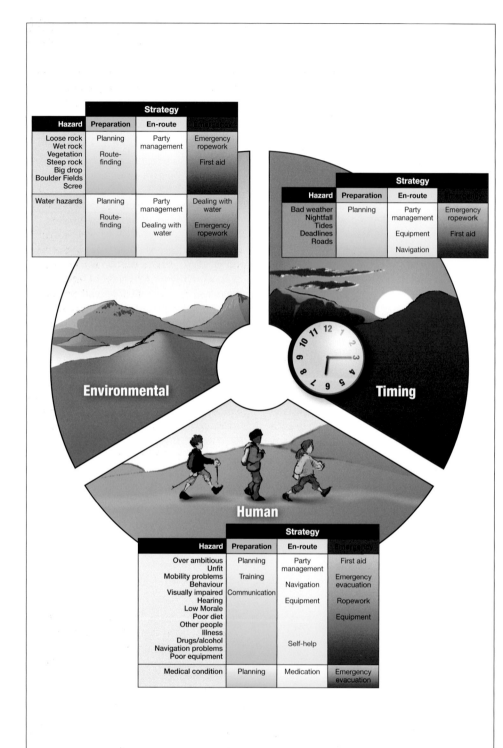

Environmental

	Strategy		
Hazard	**Preparation**	**En-route**	**Emergency**
Loose rock Wet rock Vegetation Steep rock Big drop Boulder Fields Scree	Planning Route-finding	Party management	Emergency ropework First aid
Water hazards	Planning Route-finding	Party management Dealing with water	Dealing with water Emergency ropework

Timing

	Strategy		
Hazard	**Preparation**	**En-route**	**Emergency**
Bad weather Nightfall Tides Deadlines Roads	Planning	Party management Equipment Navigation	Emergency ropework First aid

Human

	Strategy		
Hazard	**Preparation**	**En-route**	**Emergency**
Over ambitious Unfit Mobility problems Behaviour Visually impaired Hearing Low Morale Poor diet Other people Illness Drugs/alcohol Navigation problems Poor equipment	Planning Training Communication	Party management Navigation Equipment Self-help	First aid Emergency evacuation Ropework Equipment
Medical condition	Planning	Medication	Emergency evacuation

FIGURE 7.05   HAZARD COMPONENTS

Balancing interest and safety

All adventure involves a reasonable level of calculated risk. When there are fewer experienced members within a group the leader needs to maintain an enjoyable balance between interest and safety. However changing circumstances can upset this equilibrium: the leader needs to recognise early warning signs and take appropriate action to protect the party from any potential risk. Leaders need to consider carefully all the possible options for ensuring their own and their clients' safety. Consideration should be given to individuals with regard to their skills, abilities and frame of mind. Different approaches will be needed with the wide variety of groups and individuals that could be involved. It is important for any leader to develop a good understanding of the strengths and weaknesses of any particular group or individual in their care. Time should be spent talking to and watching people in order to gain this information. This will allow for a much more informed approach as to what people are capable of and how best to manage them in risk situations. Developing a good team spirit and a mutual support within the trekking group can greatly support the role of the leader.

When briefing a group about hazards it is important to understand how use of language and tone of voice can affect an individual's perception of how serious a particular hazard is. It is often better to highlight the coping strategy rather than the hazard, for instance 'let's move carefully here' rather than 'don't slip or you may injure yourself'.

7.3.3 Timing

In some circumstances effective planning and time management is required to ensure certain hazards are avoided such as crossing rivers at an appropriate time of day to avoid high water, reaching camps before nightfall, trekking over a high pass before the seasons change *(see Figure 7.05)*.

ground in front but also farther afield. Adopting a proactive approach to assessment of terrain is always preferable to a reactive one. Where real risk exists it is important to take steps to reduce this to an acceptable level. Experience and careful route choice in a variety of terrain is essential in being able to make good decisions in these situations. Developing a team's ability to identify hazards and manage the level of risk will greatly support any leader.

7.4 A practical risk management system

Due to the diverse nature of the potential environments encountered while trekking it is difficult to detail every hazard that could be confronted within the scope of this book. However the principles of risk assessment, planning, observation, negotiating and managing hazards are generic processes that can be used in a variety of situations.

Where possible try to anticipate the hazards in advance allowing the option for dealing with them beforehand. As you travel, try to use all the available information, consider not only the

7.5 Specific hazards

Trekking often takes place in a wide variety of different environments, indeed on any one particular trip it may be possible to travel through very different types of terrain from mountain to desert or jungle to city. Naturally these are different environments and while they may have a number of hazards in common there will be plenty that are specific to those places. Once again experience and research will allow for better preparation for any specific environment and its associated hazards.

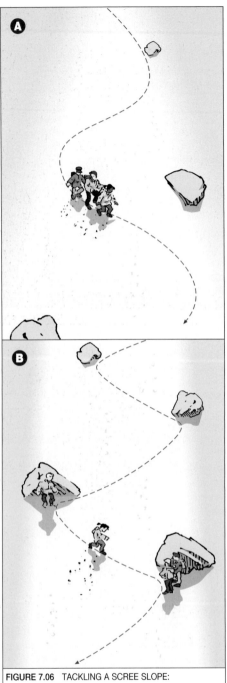

FIGURE 7.07 WALKING UP LOOSE GROUND
ILLUSTRATING ZIG ZAG   Photo: www.pyb.co.uk

7.6 Loose terrain

In many trekking environments the loose nature of the terrain can present a very real hazard. This can be made worse by the effects of the weather, increasing the potential for rock fall or mud slides. Some maps can indicate these areas; however in these situations consider changing the route or perhaps delaying until the risk level reduces.

7.6.1 Loose rock

Loose rock is a common hazard and consideration should always be given to potential rock fall from above when travelling through or below steep ground. Where dangerously loose ground exists avoidance, where possible, is the best course of action and if no alternatives are available moving quickly across the area, perhaps spreading out, will help to minimise the risk. Some areas are clearly run-out zones for rock fall or avalanche debris, and may display obvious signs such as scaring on rocks, mud slides and debris flows. This type of terrain is often the most difficult to move over and if other people or animals are above rock fall triggered by them can be a real threat. Always be mindful of the terrain and people around you especially in the large mountains where it is good to consider the 'bigger picture'

FIGURE 7.06 TACKLING A SCREE SLOPE:
A EASY BUT LOOSE SCREE, PARTY STAYS TOGETHER
B AWKWARD LOOSE SCREE, PARTY RE-GROUPS
UNDER PROTECTIVE BOULDER

FIGURE 7.08   BEAR-PROOFING A CAMP IN NORTHERN ONTARIO   Photo: John Cousins

when assessing any risk. If anything is dislodged it is always worth shouting 'below', or something to alert others so they can take avoiding action.

Some trekking routes may involve travel on **moraines**, which by their nature tend to be very loose and difficult to move over. Paths on this terrain often change and are greatly affected by rain and snow especially. Sometimes the paths are well marked and easy to follow, but where the slope is active the path line can change frequently, and careful route choice is necessary to minimise time and exposure.

7.7 Plants

The plant life encountered on some trips can be very beautiful but may also be hazardous to touch or brush against. Foraging for food in the wild can be a great source of fun and education; however common sense and care needs to be exercised. If in doubt do not pick or eat anything you are unable to identify. Food near a trail and especially low down could be dangerous due to animals excreting in the area. Fruits and fungi are often difficult to identify and the consequences of eating something poisonous can be extremely serious *(see Figure 7.09)*.

FIGURE 7.09   MONK'S HOOD   Photo: www.pyb.co.uk

7.8 Animals

Wild animals should be treated with great caution. Trek support animals need to be given a wide berth and care with the use of flash photography is wise. When passing pack animals always try standing on the up-hill side of them to avoid being knocked off the trail and do not try to cross bridges against them!

FIGURE 7.10 BUG-PROOF SUIT   Photo: John Cousins

Contact with 'domestic' animals such as cats and dogs should be avoided as in many countries they may be carriers of diseases such as rabies. In some areas bears, large cats and other large predators can be a problem. Many national parks have strict guidelines and codes of practice for visitors, warning them of the dangers and advising them how to protect against any possible encounter. Research beforehand will allow time for the organisation of any specialist equipment required to deal with these issues. This could amount to anything from animal-proof food storage bags to pepper sprays or guns (see Figure 7.08).

Smaller animals and in particular insects may be carriers of diseases that can be passed on through contact. Ticks, leeches and mosquitoes all have a reputation for biting and infecting their host.

Ensure the appropriate steps are taken to reduce the risk of being bitten by using good quality insect repellent on a regular basis, especially on areas of exposed skin. Some insects will bite through certain types of clothing so make sure repellent is also worn underneath garments. Clothing, tents and fabrics can be proofed with an array of different soaps, washes and sprays enhancing the level of protection. Elasticated cuffs on shirts and trousers can help prevent access under any clothing worn and should be considered in areas where there is a high risk. Hats and insect nets for use during the day and at night may be the only way to prevent against bites and make for a more pleasurable experience (see Figure 7.10).

Snakes, spiders and scorpions are surreptitious creatures and generally more aware of humans than we are of them. Avoid walking through habitats where these creatures may live, stick to well trodden routes as it is less likely that they will frequent these areas and at camp ensure tents are closed to prevent access of unwanted visitors. In areas of high risk check sleeping bags, boots, clothing and any other equipment that could provide shelter for such creatures before using it.

With insect bites it is important to treat and protect against any further infection as soon as possible. Monitor for any further signs or symptoms of development as this could be an indication of problems that could require medical assistance. In the event of a more serious animal bite it will be important to seek medical attention as soon as possible. Prior training in how to deal with these situations will help with the short-term care of any patient. If possible take any photos or note down a description of the creature involved to help with its identification. It is also useful to draw a line around the bite on the skin. It will help demonstrate how far the infection

FIGURE 7.11   A ROPE BEING USED TO SAFEGUARD A STEP IN TREKKING TERRAIN   Photo: www.pyb.co.uk

has spread. This is particularly important when dealing with a poisonous bite so as to ensure the correct treatment is given. Occasionally signs or symptoms of infection lie dormant for some time and only manifest themselves after returning home. In these cases it is important to consult a doctor as soon as possible.

7.9 Rope skills for trekking

The possibility that a rope might be required to deal with an unexpected situation is one of the defining characteristics of mountain terrain, and this is a skill expected of any mountain leader but also anyone venturing into steeper terrain. While the main purpose for using a rope might be to provide physical protection to party members where a potential slip cannot be safeguarded by other means, there are many other situations when trekking where its use might be appropriate. To protect steep rock steps, retrieve equipment and people from difficult places, solve problems presented by terrain and fixed equipment are all examples of such situations *(see Figure 7.11)*.

Judgement and experience is the key to making good decisions regarding where, when and how to employ the rope. Simple solutions often prove to be the most effective and appropriate ways of ensuring the risk is managed safely *(see Figure 7.12)*.

 Leader's Information

Briefing before technical ground
It is important for leaders in these situations to give a short calm briefing about what is going to happen, and then reassure people once they are on the rope. A group or individual will respond well to the calm reassurance from a leader who appears to be confident and in control of the situation. It is normal to safeguard people one at a time on the rope, this makes communication and management of the situation easier.

7.9.1 Techniques
It is important to have experience of a range of techniques that can then be employed in the wide variety of situations. The basic rope work skills required for safeguarding people up, down or across any ground can be practiced in advance on less serious terrain.

The key skill of choosing good quality anchors underpins the safety of many situations where a rope is used. Anchors need to be checked carefully to ensure they are solid and safe to use. Time spent conducting both visual and physical checks are a necessary part of this process. Where an appropriate anchor is available it is normal to combine this with a sitting braced stance. The security of this system is increased

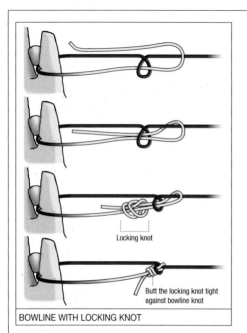

Locking knot

Butt the locking knot tight against bowline knot

BOWLINE WITH LOCKING KNOT

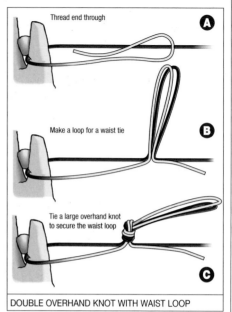

Thread end through

Make a loop for a waist tie

Tie a large overhand knot to secure the waist loop

A

B

C

DOUBLE OVERHAND KNOT WITH WAIST LOOP

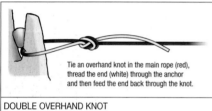

Tie an overhand knot in the main rope (red), thread the end (white) through the anchor and then feed the end back through the knot.

DOUBLE OVERHAND KNOT

FIGURE 7.12 METHODS OF ATTACHING AN ANCHOR

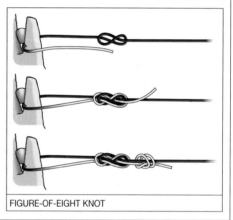

FIGURE-OF-EIGHT KNOT

FIGURE 7.13 A LEADER MANAGING A TREKKING GROUP WHEN USING A ROPE TO SAFEGUARD A STEP/ SECTION　　　　　　Photo: www.pyb.co.uk

when the belayer is sat braced behind a solid rock or section of terrain. The use of a waist belay will keep the rope tight around the person ascending or descending and in the event of a slip the extra friction created using this method will prevent a further fall.

If no solid anchors are available the belayer should endeavour to create a good stance bracing their heels into the ground and sitting well back from the edge. This has two advantages; first people tied to the rope are safeguarded away from the edge, and second the ground in front of the belayer will help to create more friction on the rope and so reduce the load felt by the belayer.

FIGURE 7.14   TIED-OFF ANCHOR

FIGURE 7.15   TIED-OFF PERSON

It is important especially in these situations that the A B C principle is followed: Anchor, Belayer, Climber, in a straight line and with everything tight.

7.9.2 Direct belays

On occasions it may be appropriate to use the anchor to provide the friction rather than incorporating a body belay. This could be the case when using a karabiner directly attached to a piece of fixed equipment for belaying. In these situations considerable experience and judgement is called for as a poor choice of anchor could result in catastrophic failure with serious consequences.

When considering an anchor for use as a direct belay, additional checks should be made to ensure the rope will run freely without jamming or slipping. There may be situations where even though a direct belay is being used the belayer may need to consider safeguarding themselves, especially when belaying in exposed situations (see Figure 7.18).

A sling and a few screwgate karabiners are useful additions to carry with a rope. These small, lightweight items can increase the options available when considering the skills required when dealing with a situation. The addition of these items can also make using fixed equipment far easier (bolts, pegs metal staples, spikes, etc.).

Protecting a traverse can involve using a range of improvised techniques to provide security. With an experienced and capable group this may require nothing more than a good briefing and supervision to cross the hazard. Some individuals may require more assistance and security. This can be done with a sling or rope tied snug around the waist with a short tail

FIGURE 7.16   THE POTENTIAL CONSEQUENCES OF BELAYING OUT OF LINE

FIGURE 7.17 **A** USE OF SINGLE ANCHORS, BOLTS **B** ATTACHING THE ROPE DIRECTLY TO FIXED EQUIPMENT
C SAFEGUARDING AN EQUIPPED TRAVERSE

Photos: www.pyb.co.uk

FIGURE 7.18 LEADER IS SAFEGUARDED ON AN
EDGE WHILE BELAYING THE ROPE FOR A CLIENT
DESCENDING A SECTION OF STEEP GROUND

and knot used to attach to the cable. It is important to keep the tail used for attachment relatively short to avoid it becoming a trip hazard and to reduce the potential for any shock loading in the event of a slip *(see Figure 7.17c)*.

7.9.3 Exposure

Some mountain trekking routes pass through very exposed terrain, and for some this is a new and threatening experience which more experienced friends and leaders may have to deal with. These situations can cause feelings of vertigo and have a detrimental affect on movement. Staying close to the person to provide reassurance and encouragement will reduce the effects generated by their surroundings *(see Figure 7.22)*;

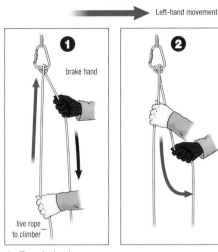

Left-hand movement   Right-hand movement

1 Feed slack through the HMS with a hand on each rope

2 Move the non-brake hand onto the dead rope below the brake hand

3 Slide the brake hand back up the rope

4 Move the non-brake hand back to the live rope

FIGURE 7.19   OPERATING AN ITALIAN HITCH

however as a last resort the use of the rope can provide both physical and psychological security.

7.10 Fixed equipment

On many routes in the mountains of Europe and to a lesser extent the greater ranges, equipment is in place to make passage easier and safer. It is common on some walking routes to cross, climb or descend a short difficult or exposed section of ground and find some form of fixed equipment. The type and style of this equipment varies greatly from one location to the next. In some places equipment is provided when it isn't really needed, and in others where it would be useful it is absent. Guide books, maps and advice from local people may help to plan for such situations (*see Figure 7.17, 7.21 and 7.23*).

When confronted with a section of fixed equipment there are various considerations to make before using it. It is important only to use the equipment if it makes travel easier and safer. A common sense approach is to assume any fixed equipment is poor until a check has proven otherwise. Therefore check the integrity of any

FIGURE 7.20   USING A DIRECT BELAY AND ITALIAN HITCH   Photo: www.pyb.co.uk

FIGURE 7.21 PROVIDING HELP AND SECURITY BY CLOSE SPOTTING
Photo: www.pyb.co.uk

FIGURE 7.22 ASCENDING FIXED LADDERS IN BUGABOO NATIONAL PARK
Photo: John Cousins

fixed equipment before use. The equipment involved may take the form of anything from a short length of rope tied to a tree, to sections of bolts linked by cable, and occasionally metal spikes with foot plates fixed to the rock.

A check should be methodical and will often involve a careful visual inspection of the complete section to be used. Checking the rock the anchors are attached to is also important; look for cracks and perhaps flaking which may indicate a poor fixing. The stability of any rock can be tested with a combination of visual and physical checks. When physically checking, a simple tap of the rock with one hand while feeling for movement with the other, as well as watching and listening, works well to identify any suspect anchors.

Sometimes short sections of fixed gear are missing or too damaged to use, and this can mean that some improvisation is needed. This may take the form of adding a sling to pull on, or using a rope to replace a section of missing cable.

FIGURE 7.23 FIXED CHAINS ON AN ALPINE PATH
Photo: www.pyb.co.uk

FIGURE 7.24   AN EXPOSED PATH IN THE BRENTA DOLOMITES   Photo: Bob Kinnaird

(ⓧ) Leader's Information

Managing groups on fixed equipment

Having made sure the equipment is safe to use, the leader should brief the group appropriately. As well as demonstrating how to hold a chain or pass an anchor point, highlight the requirement for skillful footwork rather than over reliance on equipment. When on a protected traverse having just one person in each section of chain at a time means they are not too close together, and any movement of the chain does not affect others.

When descending or ascending a steep equipped section of terrain it is often advantageous for the group leader or most experienced member to check the security of any fixed gear. This enables the leader

to make an assessment of the difficulty, and identify safe places for regrouping.

Any metalware should be inspected carefully, paying particular attention to attachment points, and the cables, chains or ropes linking these together. Some cables are covered with a plastic sleeve which protects both the cable from wear and hands from damage. On many more recent sections the bolts are linked with sections of chain or cable. When handling these it is worth wearing a thin pair of gloves to protect against injury from worn or burred cable. Also bear in mind that multi-day treks will mean carrying larger rucksacks.

FIGURE 7.25   TYPICAL SUSPENSION BRIDGE CROSSING IN TORRES DEL PAINE   Photo: Helen Barnard

7.11 Water hazards

Throughout the course of a trek it is possible to encounter all manner of water hazards from streams and rivers to lakes and marshes. Even hotel swimming pools and beaches at some destinations can present issues. **When planning and especially if there is a likelihood of confronting any water hazards consider acquiring both training and suitable equipment to deal with such issues.**

7.11.1 Lakes
There can be nothing more refreshing at the end of a hard day's trekking than to have a quick dip in a lake. Caution should be exercised, particularly in deep water where it becomes difficult to assess the depth, content and temperature of the water. Often mountain lakes are much colder than anticipated and people have been known to drown due to cramp seizing the muscles *(see Figure 7.26).*

7.11.2 Marshes
Many foreign maps do not mark marshes and boggy ground in the same way as found on UK maps. This can make planning and anticipation of such hazards difficult; however observing the vegetation while trekking provides the best indication to these areas. These hazards can be difficult to assess and negotiate, often with hidden issues such as holes, subterranean streams and animals. In many developing countries the stagnant nature of the water found in marshland areas can also present a risk from disease.

7.11.3 Tidal
Treks may start or finish at the coast so a word on the hazards of tidal regions is not misplaced at this point. The nature of the tide and sea in any particular location will be unique and should therefore be treated with caution, especially by people with little experience of the ways of the sea. Tidal ranges and currents are very specific to one location and coupled with the prevailing weather conditions can be very difficult to predict. Without good local knowledge it will be difficult to determine the depth and nature of the seabed and if any undercurrents exist that may catch people unawares. The marine life that inhabits certain locations may also present a risk, once again highlighting the need for research and caution.

FIGURE 7.26   A BREAK FROM THE TREK BUT NOT FROM POTENTIAL HAZARD   Photo: Outlook Expeditions

7.12 River crossings for trekkers

Crossing water is a relatively common challenge facing trekkers in many areas of the world. Without doubt a 'wet' crossing represents a high level of risk to the participants and should not be undertaken if a 'dry', safer alternative is practical. Any leader must conduct a dynamic risk assessment and be confident that the benefits outweigh the risks.

The time of year can have a profound affect on water levels; the monsoon season could see a trek having to make a major detour or having to wait a considerable time while the waters receded enough for a safe crossing. While this may be localised and difficult to plan for, any advanced consideration given could save the itinerary. In practice once all possibilities of a dry crossing or waiting have been discounted a wet crossing is the only option and has to be carefully planned and managed to ensure safety.

FIGURE 7.27   SIMPLE STREAM CROSSING
Photo: Helen Barnard

(Y) Leader's Information

Water safety training

A number of organisations have developed modules on supervising groups along rivers, lakes and the sea making this valuable additional training for leaders taking groups to some environments.

FIGURE 7.28   CABLEWAY CROSSING ACROSS A LARGER RIVER   Photo: Mike Rosser

FIGURE 7.29   TENSIONED CABLEWAY CROSSING IN
PATAGONIA   Photo: Iain Peter

7.12.1 Selection of a crossing point – using bridges

By far the easiest way to cross any section of water is to use a bridge, but in some countries this may present problems. It is possible to encounter a wide variety of bridge types when travelling. Many will be constructed by locals from local materials and may appear very flimsy and uninspiring. Do not assume that all crossing points are safe; try to make an assessment of the structure before crossing. Observing others crossing can often provide a steer as to how the bridge will perform and how best to cross safely. Some bridges are built to support just one person and overloading is likely to increase the hazard level as well as making movement more difficult. If trekking in remote or less frequented areas and particularly in early season more care will be required as the structure may have deteriorated over the winter/wet season *(see Figure 7.29).*

Tensioned wire crossings are found in many areas and provide a small basket which transports one person. Care needs to be taken to ensure people are properly secure and that hands and equipment are kept well away from any moving pulleys or wheels. Care is also needed to co-ordinate the pulling of the laden basket from one side to the other. Excessive speed can cause difficulties and danger.

7.12.2 Wet options

Water courses will have daily fluctuations in levels; glacial streams will be higher in the afternoon and rainforest streams will rise after heavy rain (normally late afternoon). Predicting water levels in many places can be difficult as rainfall and glacial melting in other areas can have a profound affect on your location.

Having decided crossing the river is the best option a thorough inspection to find the best crossing point is essential and the following factors must be carefully considered.

FIGURE 7.30 **A** LOW WATER IN THE MORNING **B** HIGH WATER IN THE AFTERNOON   Photo: Mal Creasey

- The perception of the water may lead you to believe that it does not present a significant hazard; however it will often be colder and the currents stronger than anticipated. It is worth noting that the body loses heat 20–30 times quicker in water than air; this can be considerably more in swift water and increases the potential for hypothermia even with quick immersion.
- Unless using specialist gear, mountain clothing and equipment is generally not designed for being in water. Once soaked it can become heavy and very restrictive.
- Downstream obstacles may pose a threat, and a thorough examination of the area below the crossing point essential.
- The area selected should be free of obstructions, submerged or otherwise, such as large boulders or fallen trees. Avoid high banks and make sure the exit point is reasonable, with good access along both banks.
- The current is usually strongest on the outside of bends. Here you are likely to find undercut banks and deep, fast flowing water.
- The riverbed should be as even as possible, of uniform depth and free of boulders, rock outcrops or clinging mud. Shingle makes an ideal surface.
- Do not rely on always being able to cross a river at a particular point.

A rise in water level can change a safe crossing into a dangerous one. To some extent the selection of the best crossing point will be influenced by the limitations of the equipment carried and the experience of the party. If the crossing is to be safeguarded by a rope the length of the rope will be a limiting factor.

FIGURE 7.31   A SERIOUS RIVER CROSSING IN GREENLAND   Photo: Nigel Williams

FIGURE 7.32 FOOT ENTRAPMENT

FIGURE 7.33 DEFENSIVE SWIMMING

Finally, consider the outcomes if someone were to fall in and be swept away. How can they be safeguarded, if at all? *If in doubt do not cross; try to choose a more suitable place or wait for more favourable conditions.*

7.12.3 Preparations before crossing

Brief everyone carefully on the procedures, making sure that everyone knows exactly what their roles are. Agree on the order of crossing and arrange the party according to size and strength. Work through a dry run on the bank to confirm the group understands the process and how they are to communicate; a clear simple system of verbal/visual communication is essential as rivers can be noisy places *(see Figure 7.31)*.

Some points to consider before making a crossing.

- Rucksacks should be loosened off with the waist straps undone, making them easier to remove in the event of a swim. Carrying a load when crossing in the water can present problems with balance and co-ordination and increase the chance of falling in. It is prefer-

able to seek other ways of transporting equipment across separately. A dry bag will help to keep the contents dry along with the addition of buoyancy should the rucksack end up in the water *(see Figure 7.31)*.

- Clothing should be fastened and all pockets closed with any loose items removed and stored safely.
- Boots should always be worn to protect the feet when crossing although removing socks to put back on after crossing would be advisable. Keeping gaiters on will help to minimise the cold on the legs and secure any loose clothing around the feet that could be a potential trip hazard.

7.12.4 River-crossing techniques

Moving water can be extremely powerful, requiring very little depth to compromise your balance. In the event of being swept off balance you should remember the following.

- *Foot entrapments:* If swept off your feet do not try to stand up in the flow as placing your feet on the riverbed could cause a foot to become trapped. In this situation the water pressure may push you over holding you in the current or worst still under the surface of the water *(see Figure 7.32)*.
- *Defensive swimming position:* Try to adopt a position with your feet facing downstream on the surface, legs slightly bent, thus allowing you to see what is approaching. Using a backstroke movement try and swim to the most appropriate bank to exit *(see Figure 7.33)*.

The methods highlighted below will help to maintain balance as well as reduce the effect from the moving water.

FIGURE 7.34   LINE ASTERN

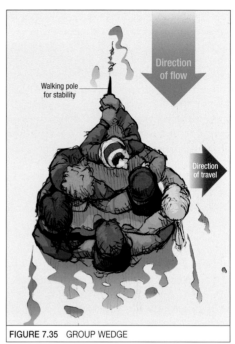

FIGURE 7.35   GROUP WEDGE

7.12.6 Line astern

This is where a group of three or more takes up position as shown in the diagram, each member facing upstream and holding on to the person in front *(see Figure 7.34)*. The leader could, if possible, use a pole for support. The whole line should progressively move sideways, each step being co-ordinated by the leader.

7.12.7 Group wedge

Similar to line astern, but the position of the group members creates a triangle (wedge) thereby creating an eddy behind them. This can be very useful for deflecting the effect of the flow away allowing other group members to gain more shelter.

7.12.8 Crossing with the aid of the rope

Mountaineering rope, being manufactured from nylon, is negatively buoyant and it sinks causing a risk of snagging. A purposely-designed floating

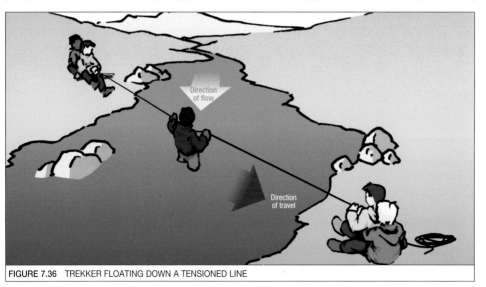

FIGURE 7.36   TREKKER FLOATING DOWN A TENSIONED LINE

rope and maybe even a buoyancy aid should be considered if planning many river crossings.

The use of a rope should really only be considered when all the above options have been explored. Essentially the rope provides support, although the perception is that it provides security. You may tend to use the rope where the water is deeper or the risk of being swept off your feet is a consideration. The rope also provides a much easier way to transport rucksacks across the river.

The length of rope will be a limiting factor and for many river crossing situations a 50m rope will be more appropriate; even then this may not be sufficient. There are some basic key points to remember.

- Do not tie onto the rope
- Keep a clean line – do not tie any knots in the rope
- Avoid tying the rope to anchors
- Try to keep the rope out of the water
- Keep the rope tight

7.12.9 The tensioned diagonal

Employing simple techniques is the most effective way to ensure safe management. Using a tensioned downstream diagonal offers a simple solution, using the force of the water to power a diagonal movement along a line. Where possible the rope should be kept out of the water and the angle to the flow must be less than 45°. The amount of rope roughly needed to cross a river 10m wide would be 30m and as a basic rule, the more rope being used the more acute the angle. Good teamwork and communication is required to hold the rope tight.

Each person crossing holds the rope on the downstream side to avoid entanglement. In fast flowing water, it is likely that the crosser will have to hand-over-hand down the rope with feet floating behind. Who makes the first crossing and where does the leader fit in?

 Leader's Information

Support team crossing rivers
Leaders of groups will also have to consider how to manage the support team and pack animals when contemplating any form of crossing.

7.13 Road hazards

Travel can be the most hazardous part of any trip particularly in the developing world. The approach to transport and personal safety is often alarming for those used to western standards. So using a reputable in-country agent is important and negotiating the type and quality of transport to be used is crucial. If travelling using public transport then this can be more of a lottery. Buses in poor condition and heavily overloaded are commonplace, so it is wise to look over any vehicle before boarding. Care with baggage to avoid loss or theft when travelling is also needed. It's a good idea to make your baggage look as old and similar to any local bags as possible and don't let it out of your sight!

Weather

THE MATTERHORN FROM ST. LUC

The weather can greatly affect our plans and preparations for a trek so being aware of the seasons and the best time to go is crucial. Knowing where to access weather information and understanding it will help in the decision-making and the planning process, which will also determine the type of clothing and equipment that will be required.

We know the weather of western Europe is very different from that of Southern India, that the temperature in an Alpine resort will not be the same in December as it is in July and that there is a particular 'climbing season' in the Himalaya. All these statements are expressions of the fact that weather at a particular place and time is always set in the broader contexts of climate and the cycle of the seasons.

In high and mid latitudes, the winter and summer seasons are very distinct in terms of both temperature and daylight hours. Seasons in lower latitudes are always warm unless up in the mountains, and day and night are of a similar length. In many of these locations seasons are defined by patterns of rainfall (dry seasons and wet seasons). In some areas near the equator there are two wet seasons, for example the 'long rains' and 'short rains' in Kenya.

The climates of the world are classified on the basis of their average seasonal patterns of both temperature and rainfall. It becomes difficult to match zones of climate to latitude because distribution of climates is complicated by many other geographical factors. As an example altitude is one such factor. Mount Kilimanjaro is only a few degrees south of the equator yet due to its altitude of just less than 6000m it is often snow-capped throughout the year.

In general terms, the climate of a region may be thought of as the average conditions that are experienced in that area over a long period of time. The weather experienced is determined by the precise state of the atmosphere at a particular time and place. Weather is always changing and the climate in different parts of the world is a combination of all the factors that affect the weather in any particular locality.

Climates vary from place to place because of five main factors.

- Latitude (distance from the equator)
- Altitude (height above sea level)
- Topography (surface features)
- Distance from oceans and large lakes
- The circulation of the atmosphere

Latitude

The atmospheric processes that show themselves through the weather are powered from the energy delivered by the sun. Radiation reaching the atmosphere and earth's surface creates a complicated sequence of processes that determine the ways in which the air, oceans and land heat up or cool down.

The sun continually sends radiation into space in the form of visible light, infrared (heat) rays and ultraviolet rays. About 30 per cent of the radiation that reaches the earth's atmosphere

FIGURE 8.01 LONG DISTANCE VIEW OF KILIMANJARO

Photo: Iain Peter

is reflected back into space, mostly by clouds, while the remaining 70 per cent is absorbed by the atmosphere and the earth's surface. Due to the curvature of the earth, the share of solar radiation that a specific place receives depends on its latitude.

At latitudes between the tropic of Cancer (23.5°N) and the tropic of Capricorn (23.5°S) the sun is directly overhead at noon twice a year. In this region around the equator the sun's rays are almost perpendicular to the earth's surface. The radiation that reaches the atmosphere is therefore at its most intense. At higher latitudes, the rays strike the surface at an angle and are therefore less intense.

In the tropical latitudes, there is little difference in the amount of solar heating between summer and winter. Average monthly temperatures therefore do not change much during the year. In middle latitudes, from the tropic of Cancer to the Arctic Circle and from the tropic of Capricorn to the Antarctic Circle, solar heating is considerably greater in summer than in winter. In these latitudes, summers are warmer than winters and therefore the seasons more distinct.

In high latitudes, north of the Arctic Circle and south of the Antarctic Circle, the sun never rises during large portions of the year. Therefore the contrast in solar heating between summer and winter is extreme. Summers are cool to mild, and winters are bitterly cold.

Terrain/topography

The higher a place is, the colder it is. Air temperature drops an average of about 6.5°C per 1000m. The temperature of the air determines how much precipitation falls as snow, rather than rain. Even in the tropics, it is not unusual for mountain tops to be snow-covered.

The surface features of the earth influence the development of clouds and precipitation. As humid air sweeps up the slopes of a mountain range, the air cools, and clouds form. Eventually, rain or snow falls from the clouds. Some of the rainiest places on earth are on windward slopes. As winds blow down the opposite slopes, known as the leeward slopes, the air warms, and clouds thin out or vanish. Leeward slopes of mountain ranges are therefore dry. In addition, a rain shadow (dry area) may stretch hundreds of kilometres downwind of a mountain range.

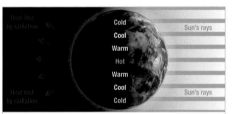

FIGURE 8.02 HOT AND COLD AIR MASS DISTRIBUTION AROUND THE GLOBE

FIGURE 8.03 THE GUILLATIRI VOLCANO, RESERVA DE LAS VICUNAS   Photo: Outlook Expeditions

Oceans

Oceans and large lakes make the air temperature less extreme in places downwind of them. An ocean or lake surface warms up and cools down more slowly than a land surface. Thus, between summer and winter, the temperature of the water varies less than the temperature of the land. The temperature of the water strongly influences the temperature of the air above it. Therefore, air temperatures over the ocean or a large lake also vary less than air temperatures over land. As a result, places that are immediately downwind of the water have milder winters and cooler summers than places at the same latitude but well inland.

San Francisco and St. Louis, for example, are at about the same latitude and therefore receive about the same amount of solar radiation during the year. But San Francisco is immediately downwind of the Pacific Ocean, and St. Louis is well inland. Consequently, San Francisco has milder winters and cooler summers.

8.1 Global scale circulation

The differential heating and movement of air produces a circulation with warm rising air moving toward the poles at high level with a return of cooler air to the equator at lower levels. This heat exchange prevents low latitude regions from continually heating up and high latitudes from continual cooling. However these air flows do not move in straight paths from the equator to the poles. This is because the earth's rotation causes any freely moving object or fluid to appear deflected to the right of the direction of motion in the northern hemisphere and to the left in the southern hemisphere.

This is known as the Coriolis effect and was first identified by Gustave-Gaspard de Coriolis in 1835. In the northern hemisphere this apparent force causes winds to travel clockwise around high pressure systems and anti-clockwise around low pressure systems. In the southern hemisphere this is reversed with winds travelling around high pressure systems in an anti-clockwise direction and clockwise around a low pressure system.

With conditions on a rotating earth, three circulation cells between the equator and the poles are predicted, the Hadley Cell between the equator

and latitude 30°, the mid-latitude or Ferrel Cell between latitudes 30° and 60°, and the polar cell between latitude 60° and 90°.

The intense heating of the earth's surface at the equator creates convection as the surface releases this heat via radiation to the atmosphere. The heated air gains buoyancy and easily rises into the wet tropical atmosphere. The deep convection promotes a broad area of low pressure that straddles the equator called the equatorial trough. The equatorial trough is also known as the Inter Tropical Convergence Zone (ITCZ).

As air rises above the surface it diverges near the top of the troposphere and moves toward the poles. Advancing toward the pole the air begins to converge at between about 25 and 35 degrees north and south latitude. Upper air convergence and cooling causes the air to subside in the subtropics. As the air reaches the surface, atmospheric pressure increases forming the subtropical highs. The action of sinking air over these regions prevents the uplift of air needed to produce large-scale cloud formation and precipitation. In addition, compression heating of the air as it descends causes a drop in the relative humidity of the air. Consequently air in these regions is very dry and hence coincides with the location of major deserts like the Sahara.

As the air subsides toward the surface it diverges outward from the centre of the subtropical highs. On the equator side of these subtropical highs the winds are generally light and variable. In the northern hemisphere, due to the Coriolis force, the air is turned to the right of its path as it moves outward. The pressure

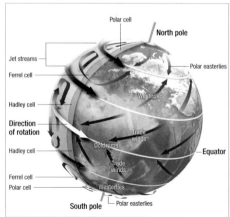

FIGURE 8.04   GLOBAL CIRCULATION MODEL SHOWING CIRCULATION CELLS AND AIR MOVEMENT

gradient between the high at 30° N and the low over the equator creates the northeast trade winds. In the southern hemisphere, the air is turned to the left of its path as it diverges from the subtropical high creating the southeast trades.

At the equator, convergence occurs between the northeast trade winds of the northern hemisphere and the southeast trade winds of the southern hemisphere creating the ITCZ. The converging trade winds form a zone of calms and weak winds with no prevailing wind direction called the "doldrums" between about 5° N and S latitude.

On the pole-ward side of the subtropical highs the air heads towards the poles but is turned to create a westerly wind pattern between 30° N and 60° N in the northern hemisphere. This wind belt is known as the westerlies with a similar westerly belt of winds found between the 30° and 60° S in the southern hemisphere.

The loss of energy at the poles creates very cold air that subsides towards the surface. This creates a dome of high pressure called the polar high. Air moving toward the equator is turned in an easterly direction creating the polar easterlies. The polar easterlies collide with the westerly wind belt at about 60° N and S, creating a broad belt of low pressure called the subpolar low. This is a zone of storms and migrating high and low pressure systems that also coincides with the location of the British Isles and one reason for explaining the variable nature of our weather.

These global wind and pressure belts are extremely important elements of the earth's climate system. They determine the geographical pattern of heat and moisture distribution and consequently the nature of the climate in any one particular place.

8.2 Kinds of climate

The earth's surface is a patchwork of climate zones. Since the early 19th century climatologists have tried to define and group theses climate zones. In 1918 St Petersberg-trained biologist Wladimir Köppen produced the first detailed classification of world climates based on vegetation cover. Köppen based his system on a region's vegetation, average monthly and annual temperature, and average monthly and annual precipitation.

The Köppen model has been modified many times. However, the basis of what the system represents is still an acceptable approach to classifying climates today *(see Figure 8.08)*.

The modified version specifies 12 climate groups.

1 Tropical wet
2 Tropical wet and dry
3 Semiarid
4 Desert
5 Subtropical dry summer

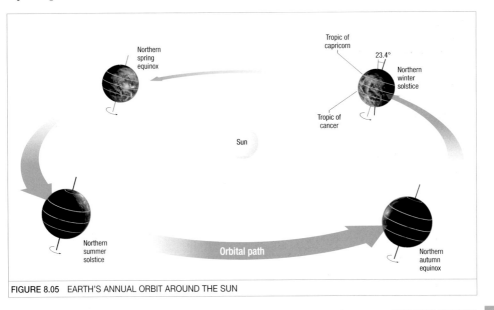

FIGURE 8.05   EARTH'S ANNUAL ORBIT AROUND THE SUN

FIGURE 8.06 A TREKKING GROUP, KAKANI, NEPAL
Photo: Steve Long

FIGURE 8.07 TREKKING IN MOUNTAIN REGIONS, SWITZERLAND
Photo: Steve Long

6 Humid subtropical
7 Humid oceanic
8 Humid continental
9 Sub Arctic
10 Tundra
11 Icecap
12 Mountain

8.2.1 Warm climates

Tropical wet climates
Tropical wet climates are hot and muggy the year round. They support dense tropical rain forests. Rainfall is heavy and occurs in frequent showers and thunderstorms throughout the year. Temperatures are high, and they change little during

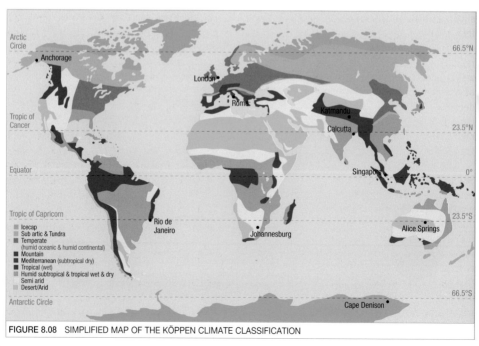

FIGURE 8.08 SIMPLIFIED MAP OF THE KÖPPEN CLIMATE CLASSIFICATION

FIGURE 8.09 TREKKING IN TUNDRA CLIMATE, ICELAND
Photo: Mike Rosser

FIGURE 8.10 TREKKING IN SUB ARCTIC CLIMATE, GREENLAND
Photo: Nigel Williams

the year. The temperature difference between day and night is greater than the temperature difference between summer and winter. Frost and freezing temperatures do not occur.

Tropical wet and dry climates

Tropical wet and dry climates occur in areas next to regions that have tropical wet climates. Temperatures in tropical wet and dry climates are similar to those in tropical wet climates, where they remain high throughout the year. The main difference between the two climates lies in their rainfall. In tropical wet and dry climates, winters are dry, and summers are wet. Generally the length of the rainy season and the average rainfall decreases with increasing latitude. Not enough rain falls in tropical wet and dry climates to support rain forests. Instead, they support savannas – grasslands with scattered trees.

Semiarid and desert climates

Semiarid and desert climates occur in regions with little precipitation. Desert climates are drier than semiarid climates. Semiarid climates, also called steppe climates, usually border desert regions. In both climate groups the temperature change between day and night is considerable. One reason for the wide swings in temperature is that the skies are clear and the air is dry. Clouds would reflect much of the sun's intense radiation during the day, slowing the rate of heating of the

air near the surface. At night, clouds and water vapour would absorb much of the earth's radiation – most of which consists of infrared rays – slowing the rate of cooling.

Subtropical dry summer climates

Subtropical dry summer climates feature warm to hot, dry summers and mild, rainy winters. These climates, sometimes called Mediterranean climates, occur on the west side of continents roughly between 30° and 45° latitude. The closer to the coast the area is, the more moderate the temperatures and the less the contrast between summer and winter temperatures.

Humid subtropical climates

Humid subtropical climates are characterised by warm to hot summers and cool winters. Rainfall is distributed fairly evenly throughout the year. Winter rainfall and sometimes snowfall is associated with large storm systems that the westerlies steer from west to east. Most summer rainfall occurs during thunderstorms and occasionally tropical storms or hurricanes. Humid subtropical climates lie on the southeast side of continents, roughly between 25° and 40° latitude.

Humid oceanic climates

Humid oceanic climates are found only on the western sides of continents where prevailing winds blow from sea to land. The moderating

FIGURE 8.11   KILIMANJARO IN THE RAINS   Photo: Mal Creasey

influence of the ocean reduces the seasonal temperature contrast so that winters are cool to mild and summers are warm. Moderate precipitation occurs throughout the year. Low clouds, fog and drizzle are common. Thunderstorms, cold waves, heat waves and droughts are rare.

Humid continental climates

Humid continental climates feature mild to warm summers and cold winters. The temperature difference between the warmest and coldest months of the year increases inland. Precipitation is distributed fairly evenly throughout the year, though many locations well inland have more precipitation in the summer. Snow is a major element in humid continental climates. Winter temperatures are so low that snowfall can be substantial and snow cover persistent. Snow cover has a chilling effect on climate. Snow strongly reflects solar radiation back into space, lowering daytime temperatures. Snow also efficiently sends out infrared radiation, lowering night time temperatures.

8.2.2 Cool climates

Sub-Arctic climates

Sub-Arctic climates have short, cool summers and long, bitterly cold winters. Freezing can occur even in midsummer. Most precipitation falls in the summer. Snow comes early in the autumn and lasts on the ground into early summer.

Tundra climates

Tundra climates are dry, with a brief, chilly summer and a bitterly cold winter. Continuous permafrost lies under much of the treeless tundra regions.

Icecap climates

Icecap climates are the coldest on earth. Summer temperatures rarely rise above freezing point. Temperatures are extremely low during the long, dark winter. Precipitation is meagre and is almost always in the form of snow.

Mountain climates

Mountain climates occur in mountainous regions. A highland climate zone is composed of several areas whose climates are like those found in flat terrain. Because air temperature decreases with increasing elevation in the mountains, each climate area is restricted to a certain range of altitude.

As a traveller trekking in the various mountainous regions of the world it is possible to encounter a range of different climates on any one trip. Indeed a climber may encounter the same sequence of climates in several thousand metres of elevation as they would if they were travelling northward for several thousand kilometres. For example, the climate at the base of a mountain might be humid subtropical, and the climate at the summit might be tundra.

8.4 Forecasts

It is worth researching the likely network coverage if any for your destination since this may allow online access to mountain weather sites and apps.

8.5 Climate

What is the climate of your intended destination? (average temperatures, precipitation, etc.) While it is very difficult to be exact about the nature of the weather in any given place weeks or months ahead it is possible to gain access to climate records that may provide an insight into average temperatures and amounts and nature of precipitation for the location being visited.

8.6 Time

When are the most favourable times to travel for the activities being undertaken? Information gained from research into the climate of a region will provide an insight as to when is the best time to visit. Depending on the nature of the activity the temperatures may need to be warmer rather than cooler or dryer as opposed to wetter.

8.7 Topography

What is the nature of the topography you will be travelling through and how will this be affected by weather (floods, mudslides, bushfires, thunderstorms)? The intended itinerary may take in a variety of terrain. Careful consideration of how the terrain may be affected by weather will allow thought for contingencies and alternative plans to be made. Potential weather extremes can have a serious effect on topography and consequently any plans made. As examples increased rainfall can contribute to both flooding and landslides, unusually dry hot periods could cause excessive snowmelt or the drying of vegetation might lead to potential fires.

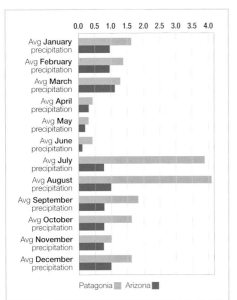

FIGURE 8.12 AVERAGE MONTHLY PRECIPITATION BETWEEN PATAGONIA AND ARIZONA, 2010

It is important to consider all the possible variables of climate that may be encountered on any one particular trip/expedition. Clothing and equipment need to be given careful consideration. It may not be possible to carry enough equipment to cope with the wide range of different climates. Planning ahead is paramount in making sure the equipment and clothing you do take can be used in a flexible way so as to cope with a range of climates. Lightweight wicking thermals can be used as t-shirts in the hotter climates but can make effective base layers for higher elevations where the climate is cooler.

8.3 Planning

Giving consideration as to the potential weather you may encounter on a trip is an inherent part of the prior planning process. Undertaking some research before departure will help to ensure people are equipped as best they can be for the weather expectations. Answering some key questions will help to gather information that can be used in making these decisions.

8.8 Phenomena

Is your destination likely to be effected by seasonal weather phenomena (monsoon, hurricanes, typhoons, etc.)? Modern day climate records allow for research into common seasonal weather phenomena that may affect a particular region. Knowing an area is subject to a monsoon or hurricane season will allow for better timing of a trip in order to avoid these periods.

8.8.1 Contingency

Despite extensive research into a destination's weather and climate it is always worth having a contingency in place to cope with a change in conditions that may affect your planned itinerary. Water and snow hazards can present considerable problems for trekkers; however it can also be difficult to predict the extent to which these will affect your route. In times of unusual weather events these could present a very serious barrier to any ongoing journey. Planning for the worst case scenario can mean you will be better prepared when faced with unseasonal changes in the weather.

8.9 Topographical weather factors

The surface features of the earth influence the weather constantly; the more pronounced these features are the greater the effect on the atmospheric conditions. Mountains can greatly affect weather to the extent of creating their own micro-climates. This often leads to localised variations in weather over short distances and can make it difficult to predict conditions. Having said this there are some basic principles to the weather in this type of terrain.

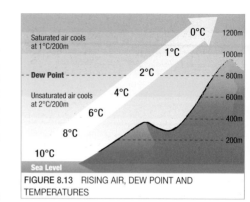

FIGURE 8.13   RISING AIR, DEW POINT AND TEMPERATURES

FIGURE 8.14   AN EXAMPLE OF FACTORS LEADING TO LOCALISED WARMING

- Temperatures will be cooler
- Precipitation will be heavier
- Winds will be stronger

8.10 Temperature

The temperature at any altitude affects walking and climbing conditions. It will influence the build up of cloud and the nature of any precipitation. In general temperature drops with an increase in altitude except in the case of an inversion. The rate at which temperature decreases with height is known as the 'lapse rate'. Dry air, which may contain moisture but where condensation into clouds has not yet occurred, will cool at a dry air lapse rate of 1°C per 100m. Once con-

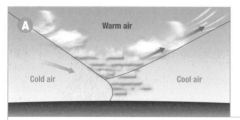

FIGURE 8.15   **A** TEMPERATURE INVERSION AND   **B** VALLEY FOG

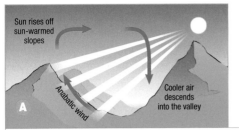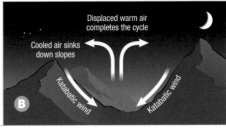

FIGURE 8.16   ILLUSTRATIONS SHOWING **A** ANABATIC AND **B** KATABATIC WINDS

densation has started the air will cool at a slower rate; saturated air lapse rate of ½°C per 100m.

8.11 Wind (anabatic and katabatic)

Topography plays an important role in influencing the speed and direction of any air movement. This is particularly the case when considering the mountain environment. The rugged nature of the terrain coupled with the atmospheric conditions can have a dramatic effect on wind speeds and directions. The result can often be dramatic localised variations. In many areas throughout the world regions have their own characteristic winds caused by the unique nature of the topography and climate in that particular location.

These specific local winds may occur at certain times of the year when conditions are favourable. They often signify a long-term change in the weather and can be associated with the changing of seasons. In some places the arrival of these winds may have some historical significance or, as in some cases, may be attributed to health problems with the local communities. Research into the climate of an area will help the understanding of these localised conditions and how they might influence your plans for any trip.

As well as influencing the prevailing winds, mountainous areas are able to generate their own microclimates. During the day, solar heating of the sunlit slopes causes the overlying air to move up-slope (termed anabatic winds). These rising currents sometimes trigger the development of convective clouds, which will produce thunderstorms if they mature. Night time land-surface radiation cools the slopes,

causing cooler, denser air to drain into the valley (termed katabatic winds). Usually light, but where landform constricts the flow the wind speed may increase significantly. The katabatic winds that blow down from the ice caps of Antarctica and Greenland (Piteraq wind) have been known to reach speeds well in excess of 150 miles per hour.

8.12 Precipitation

As well as influencing air movements, mountains can also generate and alter the nature of any precipitation. There are three categories of precipitation according to the primary mode of up-lift of the air.

- *Convective*, where warm, moisture-laden thermals rise and cool to form cumulus and cumulonimbus clouds.
- *Cyclonic*, associated with depressions whereby by one air mass lifts another.
- *Orographic*, whereby the barrier presented by the mountains forces air up and over, potentially giving rise to cloud formation/precipitation.

The nature and intensity of any precipitation will depend on temperature and topography. It may be raining low down in the valley but with cooler temperatures higher up it could mean snow. As moist air is lifted over the mountains any precipitation will tend to fall on the windward side with greater intensity than on the leeward side. It is often possible to find more favourable conditions in these locations *(see Figure 8.17)*.

FIGURE 8.17 WARM DAMP AIR BEING LIFTED OVER MOUNTAINS

8.13 Thunderstorms

FIGURE 8.18 CLOUDY FOOTHILLS AND A RAINY SUMMIT

The life cycle of a thunderstorm can be described in terms of three main stages: the developing phase during which a cumulus cloud forms; the maturing phase during which these clouds grow to form cumulonimbus producing precipitation; the dissipation phase during which the storm gradually dies down. During the developing phase moist air is lifted to start the process of cloud formation. A number of processes can cause uplift but convection is by far the most important.

In humid conditions solar heating of slopes can cause thermals to rise, carrying warm moist air into the atmosphere. As the warm air travels upwards and reaches its dew point cumulus clouds will begin to form. If convection is strong these clouds will grow taller as the updraughts continue to move air upwards. Often the development and maturation of these clouds can be monitored throughout the day.

As the storm matures the clouds will become taller and more extensive allowing less light to penetrate to lower levels giving them a very dark 'heavy' appearance. At this stage precipitation is likely in the form of exceptionally heavy rain or snow as well as hail. It is also at this stage when the intense upward and downward movement of air currents within a cloud enhance the creation of opposite electrical charges. The difference in time between an observer seeing a lightening discharge and hearing the sound of thunder can give an indication of how far away a storm might be and whether or not it is moving closer. It takes approximately five seconds for thunder to travel one mile, so by counting the number of seconds between the flash and hearing the thunder it is then possible to divide by five to give the distance.

It is worth remembering that although a storm may not pass over your location the effects of

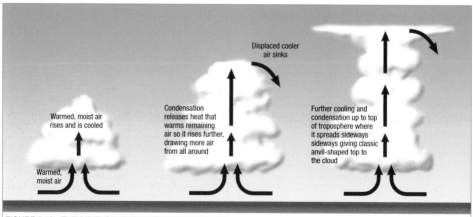

FIGURE 8.19 THE DEVELOPMENT OF THUNDERSTORMS

Warmed, moist air rises and is cooled

Warmed, moist air

Condensation releases heat that warms remaining air so it rises further, drawing more air from all around

Displaced cooler air sinks

Further cooling and condensation up to top of troposphere where it spreads sideways sideways giving classic anvil-shaped top to the cloud intense rain or snow close by may require a change of plan. The development of such storms can happen quickly and careful observation of the skies will reduce the risk of being caught in exposed places.

8.14 Observations

In remote areas we often rely on what we observe rather than a forecast to make decisions with regard to weather expectations for a particular day. With a little insight and practice it is possible to recognise changes in the weather from what we see and feel around us *(see Figure 8.18)*.

Making observations relies on nothing more than using our senses: sight, sound and feel; great for those wishing to travel light. A barometer is a useful addition to a traveller's kit list, wrist watches and GPSs are available with sensors that measure air pressure and will often display a graph showing the trend over a period of time. They also double as an altimeter, another useful tool to have as someone venturing into the high mountains. To work effectively they should be recalibrated on regular basis (at known altitudes or pressures). While it maybe good to know the exact pressure at that moment it is more useful to know the trend; whether the pressure is rising, falling or remaining steady.

Being able to forecast an improvement or deterioration in the weather should play a vital role in the decision-making process even in the absence of a forecast from a reliable source. Depressions approaching and moving across an area will bring distinct signs and changes in the weather. Observing the skies and in particular

FIGURE 8.20   LENTICULAR CLOUDS OVER RUAPEHU, NEW ZEALAND, INDICATING A CHANGE IN THE WEATHER
Photo: Mo Laurie

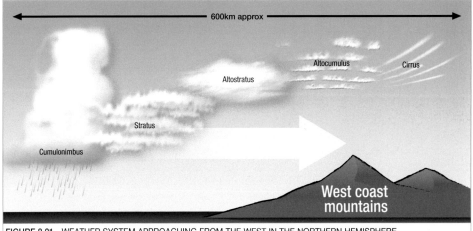

FIGURE 8.21   WEATHER SYSTEM APPROACHING FROM THE WEST IN THE NORTHERN HEMISPHERE

FIGURE 8.22 EVENING SKY IN COLORADO, INDICATING AN APPROACHING WEATHER FRONT   Photo: Iain Peter

the clouds can give useful clues as to the weather expectations for the next few hours, a day or possibly days.

Using the example of a depression crossing a location in the northern hemisphere it is possible to observe and note some of these changes *(see Figure 8.21)*.

8.14.1 Before a warm front arrives

- Wind will increase and back, there may be signs of crossed winds illustrated by the cloud formations.
- Pressure will start to drop.
- Cloud cover will increase from the prevailing direction.
- A succession of gradually descending cloud formations will be encountered.
- As clouds reach the lower levels precipitation will increase eventually becoming more continuous.
- Warm front passes over.
- The wind will veer.
- The pressure will rise.

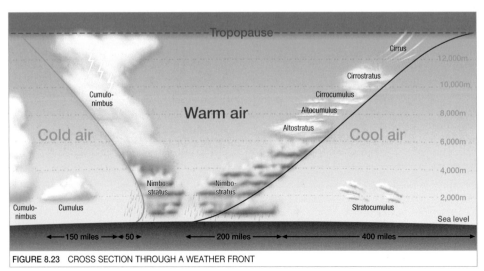

FIGURE 8.23 CROSS SECTION THROUGH A WEATHER FRONT

FIGURE 8.24 THE ARRIVAL OF A FRONT IN NORTHERN ONTARIO   Photo: John Cousins

- Low level clouds may start to fragment although this will depend on distance from the low centre.
- The dewpoint will rise illustrated by an increase in altitude of the cloud base.
- Precipitation will become less intense turning to drizzle and may cease.
- Temperature will rise; however this may be a small change and therefore sometimes diffi-cult to detect, particularly in mountainous regions.

8.14.2 Between fronts (warm sector)

A lot of the weather experienced between fronts will depend on how close your location is to the low centre and how close the warm and cold fronts are. In some circumstances the skies could clear leaving remnants of the warm front with very high level clouds trailing behind. Close to the low centre there may be very little time and change in the cloud cover before the cold front arrives *(see Figure 8.23)*.

8.14.3 Before the cold front arrives

- Wind may back slightly and strengthen.
- The pressure will begin to fall, gradually at first.
- Cloud will start to thicken.
- Precipitation may occur generally in the form of bands and showers.
- Cold front passes over.

- As a cold front passes overhead there are often very abrupt and distinctive changes in the weather.
- Wind will veer sharply and increase in speed. It may also become blustery in nature.
- The pressure will start to rise as the front moves over.
- Cloud cover is often nimbostratus; however due to the nature of a cold front there may be convective clouds produced, cumulonimbus.
- Precipitation is heavy, often with hail or thunder produced from the cumulonimbus clouds.
- Temperature will drop dramatically.

As the cold front moves away the winds initially will back and potentially become gusty and stronger for a while. As the front moves further away this will become less so. The pressure will rise and begin to steady. The precipitation will begin to cease and become more showery in nature with these becoming less intense as the front moves further away.

Online access to mountain weather sites and weather apps 3G phones.

Snow — a seasonal approach

ROLLING TERRAIN UNDER-FOOT AGAINST A BACKDROP OF SPECTACULAR SCENERY   Photo: Martin Chester

Snow-covered terrain presents a new set of challenges to any trek. It enhances the beauty of the landscape but also brings a range of hazards that require careful consideration before negotiating.

FIGURE 9.01 SNOWSHOE DESCENT IN GREENLAND Photo: Nigel Williams

Having an understanding of snow plus experience of the skills and knowledge required to operate in these conditions will make for safe and efficient travel.

From its formation snow can undergo considerable change, both as it falls through the atmosphere and after settling on the ground. The aim of this chapter is to follow the evolution of snow through a typical 'snowy season'. Given the widely dispersed areas of the globe where this is relevant, it is impossible to talk of specific months, and barely possible to consider true seasons – especially if one treks through the great perennial snowfields of the earth. It is possible to make generalisations about the phases of a snowy season – each presenting its own characteristic issues, risks, opportunities and considerations for the trekker.

The snowy season lasts from the first autumnal falls to the spring melts. Altitude and latitude will dictate how long this process takes but the stages underwriting this will be more or less the same.

make seasonal shifts to bring moisture on colder winds all leading to a lowering of the snowline. Even in the monsoon, with more precipitation and less solar warming there is potential for frost and snow (perhaps unexpected) especially at high altitudes.

Without the widespread and obvious hazards of full winter conditions, it is easy to ignore the localised yet significant dangers of this season. While there are fewer reported avalanche incidents in the autumn and early winter than in midwinter or spring, a significant risk still exists with incidents and fatalities in these conditions every year. It seems likely that many victims are

FIGURE 9.02 POORLY COVERED BOULDER SLOPES CAN BE CHALLENGING UNDERFOOT Photo: Mal Creasey

9.1 Early snowfall

9.1.1 A cold shallow snow pack

In autumn the daylight hours become shorter, and temperatures start to fall. Weather systems

FIGURE 9.03   TRAIL BREAKING IN WINTER
Photo: Caroline Hale

FIGURE 9.04   WITHOUT GOGGLES, NAVIGATION CAN BE NEARLY IMPOSSIBLE   Photo: Martin Chester

simply not considering the potential, in the assumption that there is insufficient snow to constitute a significant hazard.

Trekking through the developing snowfields of the autumn can be a frustrating business. The trekker may have to negotiate ice covered rock (verglas), accumulating frost (rime) and often insufficient snow for crampons or snowshoes to work and yet enough cover to hide all manner of hidden traps. With a slightly greater build-up of snow it can become possible to link patches of snow and ice for crampon use. Streams will start to dry up and the beds fill with drifting snow making them less useful for navigational purposes. Cornices may start to form at the edge of plateau areas. Glacial travel in particular is hazardous at this time of year. Crevassed terrain may appear safe but any fissure on the surface, be it glacial crevasse or limestone dyke, can present a considerable hidden hazard.

9.1.2. Looking after the team

The transition through cold, damp conditions to freezing is almost harder to manage than the cold dry conditions of midwinter, especially when combined with wind chill. Avoidance of any cold related injury should be prime concern in these conditions. Choosing the correct clothing, equipment and food for trekkers and porters will help to minimise the potential for hypothermia, frostbite or frostnip.

Verglas and iced up rocks present a very real hazard requiring careful negotiation. Stream crossings and rocky terrain can become more problematic in these conditions with slips easily resulting in injury. Learn to treat anything that 'looks wet' with suspicion. Step on boulders just underneath the surface of running water, and avoid frozen watercourses wherever possible *(see Figure 9.03)*.

Blizzards can result in poor visibility and even whiteout making route-finding and navigation more of a challenge. Thankfully, in early season there are still likely to be terrain features visible through the snow. A full blizzard on a high pass can transform a routine passage on a well marked trail into a serious mountaineering challenge. Consider carrying goggles or using sunglasses to protect eyes from driving snow *(see Figure 9.04)*.

Unexpected frozen vegetation and pasture can result in inadequate grazing for pack animals, and a lack of any water supply for the team. Melting snow for water and extra cooking time in cold conditions can place a greater demand on fuel usage. The autumn is no time to deny yourself a healthy margin with regards food and fuel budgets. After the storm clears, even the greyest autumnal weather can be replaced by a world of sunshine on snow. This brings the risk of snow blindness, which can be simply managed by carrying the right eyewear for the whole team (including porters) *(see **Chapter 4 Snow blindness** on page 54)*.

9.2 Early season snow and avalanche

As a consequence of snow 'settling' in steeper terrain, avalanches occur naturally throughout the snowy season. The secret is being in the right place at the right time (or rather avoiding the wrong place at the wrong time). It is therefore possible to travel through potential avalanche terrain and reduce the risks by understanding a few basic but important principles. For an avalanche to occur there are three fundamental requirements.

1 Snow
2 Terrain
3 Trigger

The **snow** pack must be inherently unstable containing a layer of snow lying on a suitable 'sliding surface'. The **terrain** must include a slope that is steep enough to allow the snow to slide, usually in excess of 25° and finally there must be something to '**trigger**' the avalanche into motion.

9.2.1 Snow pack

In many places early in the season, the snow is well anchored by the rocks and vegetation below. The danger exists in assuming this is universally the case. Furthermore, it is easy to be fooled by the appearance of lower slopes, believing there is not yet enough snow for an avalanche to occur. High above, where the first snows fall on steep perennial slopes these wind scoured surfaces may

provide an ideal sliding surface for the new layer above *(see Figure 9.05)*.

Of course, many early season snow falls are combined with the strong winds of a storm cycle, meaning there is unlikely to be a uniform distribution of snow, with substantial drifting on leeward slopes and behind obstacles.

Early season conditions are often perfect for the formation of **depth hoar**. This poorly bonded 'sugary snow' forms when the snow pack is shallow and the temperatures are cold, allowing moisture vapour from the ground to meet the comparatively colder temperatures at the surface *(see Figure 9.06)*.

The rate at which depth hoar forms is dependent on snow depth and difference in temperature. Classic conditions for the formation occur during prolonged spells of stable, cold conditions associated with high pressure in early winter. In such conditions, it is also possible for crystals to grow on the surface of the snow. In the same way that autumnal dew forms on the grass, moisture vapour in winter can crystallise on top of the snow forming characteristic feathery structures known as **surface hoar**. Surface hoar is particularly delicate and susceptible to melting by the sun and transportation by the wind. It therefore mostly tends to remain on shady slopes through periods of stable weather *(see Figure 9.07)*.

Both surface hoar and depth hoar, while beautiful and delicate, are quite pure crystalline structures and therefore difficult for nature to 'improve upon'. Once buried in the snow pack they are quite stubborn in their resistance to

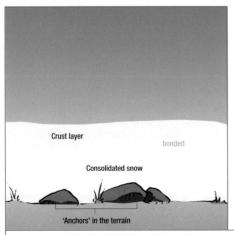

FIGURE 9.05   TWO CONTRASTING SNOW 'PROFILES' AT DIFFERENT HEIGHTS ON THE SAME MOUNTAIN

change or bonding. As such, new snow deposited on top of these crystals may be poorly bonded to the underlying surface, and seriously undermined.

It is less important to understand the process by which these crystals are produced than the need to recognise the fact that prolonged spells of cold stable weather, combined with a shallow snow pack, may be laying down fundamentally rotten foundations for the remainder of the season's snow. Thankfully, the early season weather is just as likely to include warm spells, and a good rainfall will quickly settle the snow, and help to form a well-consolidated 'base'.

The process of drifting can lead people to believe that there is little or no risk when actually the risk is significant but localised. Of course, it is important to remember that as snowfall is redistributed by wind, some areas may have enough snow to slide even though adjacent ground is left bare. It is, therefore, important to consider the second fundamental requirement; the shape of the terrain.

9.2.2 Terrain

In early season areas most likely to present a hazard, if oriented so that the wind fills them with snow, are gullies and steep high slopes in the lee of ridgelines. Gullies can often contain additional hazards, with steep drops and rocky constrictions worsening the potential consequences of a slide. Beware of snow-filled features lying above rock bands which are to feed into steep-sided areas like stream beds where the accumulation of sliding snow could be deep. Route choice is often the primary answer to reducing avalanche risk and if possible avoids areas of accumulation or terrain traps. As most avalanche victims start the avalanche themselves this will also reduce the risk of becoming a trigger.

9.2.3 Trigger

Early season avalanche incidents often result from an underestimation of the volume of snow required to produce an avalanche. This in turn leads to an overly relaxed approach to crossing potential avalanche terrain. The issue in early season is rarely the scale of the avalanche, or the risk of burial. It may only require a small avalanche to sweep you off your feet, but if that ends in a steep slide or fall onto rocky ground it can be every bit as serious as a burial.

While this is of little consolation to the one who gets avalanched, the localised nature of the trigger does at least mean that any suspect areas can be crossed one at a time with others watching. This not only reduces the potential extra load (a common trigger) on the slope, but enables your com-panions to take effective action the moment the avalanche stops.

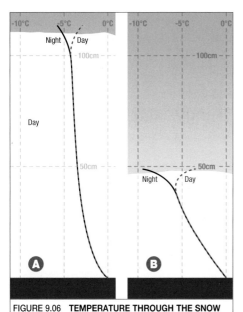

FIGURE 9.06 **TEMPERATURE THROUGH THE SNOW PACK: A** WEAK TEMPERATURE GRADIENT AND **B** VERY STRONG TEMPERATURE GRADIENT

FIGURE 9.07 SURFACE HOAR CRYSTALS
Photo: Martin Chester

FIGURE 9.08 TREKKERS ON SNOWSHOES Photo: www.pyb.co.uk

9.3 Deep midwinter – storms, wind slab and avalanches

By the time the winter snows are well established we have 'full winter conditions'. Navigation may be tricky with paths and features obscured or buried; the consequences of a simple slip may be severely punished by a traumatic slide and route choice becomes essential for safe travel through avalanche terrain *(see Figure 9.08)*.

9.3.1 Midwinter snow and avalanche

During this part of the season the underlying vegetation, scree and boulders are buried by a more substantial snow pack. These natural anchors can only secure the lowest layers of snow. What is now a smooth snow slope will increase the risk of instabilities. With the hazard becoming more widespread and more regular, this is prime avalanche season and it should be no surprise that both the scale, as well as frequency, of avalanches increases during this time. Once again, good route choice and effective group management is fundamental for safe travel, with a requirement to focus on the assessment of terrain and gradient rather than snow stability.

9.3.2 Snow pack

When travelling through the mountains at this time of year it is easy to become fixated with the snow directly underfoot and underestimate the threat from above where conditions may be significantly different. Avalanches may be enormous in scale and volume, travelling long distances from high peaks to sweep down and across the valleys below.

9.3.3 Snow-pits – a basic philosophy

Digging a pit and studying a profile of the snow is a great way to find out 'what's been going on so far this season. Unfortunately, the results vary widely from one location to another. We are commonly concerned about assessing not only the threat from the slope we are on but those that are far above us. Therefore, use the results as an educational starting point – NOT a diagnostic tool for deciding 'should I or shouldn't I?'

By this stage in the winter each significant snowfall will have settled into distinct layers. Layers tell the story of the season like the growth rings in a tree – they provide a history of an area even in the absence of avalanche bulletins or recorded measures.

FIGURE 9.09 SNOW PROFILE   Photo: www.pyb.co.uk

Look, poke and prod for hollows, weaknesses, icy layers and especially contrast. The foundations left from early season (buried depth and surface hoar – *see page 128*) can present fundamental flaws in the snow pack. Find out how they occur, and how to identify/recognise them. Of course, some buried (but significantly weak) layers are crushed thin so they are difficult to see. Stability tests can give some insight helping to discover any weak bonds that are not visible to the naked eye *(see Figure 9.09)*.

It is almost always possible to get one layer to slide on another so results are almost always ambiguous. The danger comes when trying to 'split hairs' over the results in the hope of a 'diagnosis'. Take a step back and ask what you are really deciding when faced with a 'should we or shouldn't we' decision? If you were thinking of crossing the busy M6 motorway would you really accept a 60:40 chance of crossing uninjured?

Of course there are many reasons why people suddenly take greater risks than they would normally take and these are the traps of decision making (known as heuristic traps). In the absence of any firm evidence to the contrary, it is undoubtedly safer to conclude that any ambiguous result exposes instability in the snow pack – and this should then be managed by sensible route choice and safe travel techniques.

9.3.4 Wind transportation

It is easy, on the first good day after the storm has passed, to assume that the hazard is reduced and push on in relief or desperation, but these are the days when people often get caught out.

Whether travelling on skis, snowshoes or on foot, making progress after significant snowfall can require great effort especially in soft unconsolidated snow. The danger in these conditions is that the snow pack can change in character very quickly with perhaps small but important changes to the terrain. As an example, it may be easy trekking in deep powder, in a sheltered bowl or forest, but if the ground should steepen into an area affected by the wind, the snow can make the subtle transition to soft wind-slab. If this change goes unnoticed while travelling the deep soft pile of fluff can suddenly become a homogenous sweeping mass of snow.

Another classic mistake, but thankfully trickier to make, is the misinterpretation of hard slab. When travelling through a windswept valley after a snowstorm, it is possible to encounter all kinds of textures and types of snow underfoot. As the snow firms up it is easy to think a patch of safe wind scoured snow has been found, but beware the 'hard slab' trap. This could be a densely packed drift of firm chalky wind slab with the possibility there is a hollow or poorly bonded layer beneath meaning the surface could break free as a slab avalanche.

9.3.5 Terrain

In midwinter, with regular fresh snowfalls, there is almost always some degree of instability in the snow pack. In remote areas, in the absence of any avalanche forecast information, it is always prudent to assume the worst and take defensive measures of route choice and safe travel accordingly. Anybody crossing a snowfield is potentially a trigger. One of the key skills required for safe travel is accurate interpretation of the gradient. This is simple; keep off slopes that are steep enough to slide and avoid trekking beneath potential avalanche prone slopes. This sensible approach to safe travel is supported by the remit of the International Mountain Leader scheme, which is specifically designed for 'rolling Nordic terrain'. The nature of this type of terrain, being more gentle and rolling, means there is less chance of being exposed to steep slopes (slopes more likely to avalanche).

FIGURE 9.10 TERRAIN TRAPS – WHERE THE SHAPE OF THE TERRAIN CAN COMPOUND THE RISK. **A** THREATS FROM ABOVE **B** DEBRIS IN THE PATH.

Photos: Martin Chester

9.3.6 Measuring gradient

- From the map – gradient rules and shadings
- On the ground – with an inclinometer
- On the ground – with a rough and ready 'pole test'

The shape of the ground can also have a significant impact on the chance of releasing a slab or layer of snow. Where a slab of snow bulges over a convexity in the hillside the snow pack is under tension and is fairly poorly supported from all around. The point at which a roll steepens to 30° is a classic point at which a slope will most easily release. Of course, the opposite is true in concavities like the base of a slope, gully or bowl where the angle eases. In these places, the snow is well supported, and may be more resistant to release and sliding.

In conditions of significant fresh snow and serious instability, this rule of thumb should not be relied on. In most conditions, however, it is hard to justify taking anything but the safest line, dodging steep rolls and convexities in favour of easier angles and concave bowls. This is especially true if caught out in marginal conditions (*see Figure 9.10*).

9.3.7 Terrain traps

Features that make the consequences of an avalanche significantly more serious are known as **Terrain Traps** and include the following.

- Trees
- Boulders
- Stream beds/gorges
- Flat benches

With sensible route choice and evaluation of the terrain being the primary defence in mid-winter, good visibility is imperative. As soon as you lose the ability to see the terrain, making sensible route-finding decisions can be seriously impaired (*see Figure 9.10*).

9.3.8 Trigger

Many things can trigger an avalanche. Spontaneous releases can occur with an increase in temperature, or a serious increase in the volume of snow (exacerbated by drifting in strong winds). The threat may exist down into the valley with potential for large scale releases from above. Even light additional loads (just one trekker) can be the final straw that triggers a prone slope.

Some hut Guardians dictate staggered departures in serious conditions to minimise risk – a system that could also be adopted among a small group: travelling spread out in areas of most risk.

9.3.9 Looking after the team

The key problems in the deep midwinter are the sheer volume of snow and often strong winds and drifting. Blizzard conditions are common, and can be caused by fresh snowfall, as well as strong winds 'whipping up' the existing snow from underfoot. Goggles are an essential item of equipment in the conditions. Navigation, breaking trail, and considering the avalanche hazard require full attention increasing the challenge of operating in the winter environment.

9.4 Effective planning for midwinter travel

Planning ahead for such difficult conditions can help – as decisions rehearsed in the comfort of last night's accommodation can be easier to process when confronted by adverse conditions. A useful planning tool based on Werner Munter's '3x3' model, originally designed for avalanche avoidance, can be extended to include route finding and navigation considerations – making sure everything is considered.

Consider the three important ingredients on three occasions.
• Snow and weather
• Terrain and route choice
• The group

• The night before
• First thing in the morning
• Throughout the day

This system will help plan objectives that consider avalanche, route finding and navigation issues, plus allow the flexibility for adjustments to suit changing conditions en-route.

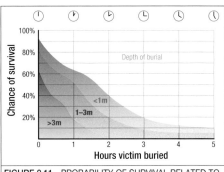

FIGURE 9.11 PROBABILITY OF SURVIVAL RELATED TO TIME AND DEPTH OF BURIAL

9.5 Avalanche – prevention is better than cure!

One only needs to glance through the gloomy statistics surrounding avalanche incidents to take the matter seriously. Around 25 per cent of people caught in an avalanche are killed by trauma. Of those surviving this, the chances of surviving burial under the snow simply plummet beyond twenty minutes. There is unlikely to be time to get help, and the only chance for survival is often companion rescue within the group. This clearly requires a member of the team to remain free of the avalanche. Rescue within the critical time frame has best chance with the practiced use of a transceiver, shovel and probe. When venturing into such terrain, carry the kit, know how to use it, and make a plan in advance *(see Figure 9.11).*

9.6 Early spring

In early spring with more daylight, the sun takes over from the wind as the most significant factor in developing the avalanche risk and consolidating the snow *(see Figure 9.12).*

Movement becomes more straightforward as the depth of the winter snow consolidates. The snow pack gives a firmer surface and icy conditions, especially in early morning. Effective use of crampons and ice axe on slopes now becomes essential for safe travel as the consequences of a slide in the wrong place can be severely punishing.

FIGURE 9.12 SNOWSHOEING IN NORWAY   Photo: www.expeditionguide.co.uk

Melting snow will increase water in streams and rivers – and where these run under the snow they can present a serious hazard. Snow bridges may well start to become more fragile during the long hot days; crossing them will require careful consideration.

9.6.1 Snow and avalanche

With the sun now higher in the sky, many more slopes receive even greater warming from the sun. Rapid melting of the snow surface during the day and refreezing overnight causes settling of the snow pack. A daily melt freeze cycle helps to consolidate the snow pack. However rapid melting during the day, especially of areas exposed to direct sunlight, will give rise to instabilities that may result in slides. Following any fresh snowfall, point release slides become more common as snow settles off rocky crags and ledges, loading the slopes below and causing them to release. Therefore it is important not to underestimate the threat from above in sunny or thaw conditions. The potential for full depth slides increases at this time of year due to increased weight of the snow pack and melt water running between the snow and the ground acting as a lubricant. It's especially important to consider this significant risk in early season treks in the greater ranges. Valley routes, tracks and trails may be open and it's tempting to make an

early start – but a substantial volume of snow can still threaten from above.

Thankfully the factors that make up these avalanches are consistent from year to year so local knowledge can be an important thing.

9.6.2 Snow pack

The transformation from fresh snow to névé occurs at a different rate in different places. Sunny and low places will make this change most quickly. In shady and high places, the snow is effectively in the 'deep freeze' and will take longer to 'go off'.

9.6.3 Terrain

Local knowledge combined with signs of previous avalanche paths can provide consistent clues to perennial problems and risks. Spring avalanches are a natural act of settling, and tend to happen in reliable and regular places. For example, notorious black spots such as found in the Annapurna sanctuary are well known to locals. Be particularly aware of terrain traps, the risk from above, and hazards below.

9.6.4 Trigger

Often the sun itself will act as the trigger. In spells of good weather there is daily warming which accelerates the settling of the snow pack. This begins as a surface effect, with refreezing

FIGURE 9.13 SUN AFFECTED SNOW WITH TRACKS
Photo: Martin Chester

FIGURE 9.14 SPRING HAS SPRUNG
Photo: Martin Chester

common overnight. This balance of effects will continue with the good weather, but if the daily warming 'wins' against the nightly freezing, instabilities will arise, and avalanches will still be likely. When the overnight temperature wins the battle for supremacy, the snow pack will refreeze and generally consolidate.

9.6.5 Looking after the team

Key problems in the spring are caused by the strong sun. Sun cream and glacier glasses are essential at this time of year for everyone as a part of the daily routine. Clothing should be carefully chosen to reflect the heat and yet be warm enough to cope with the odd snow shower.

The secret for effective travel lies in 'timing the day' carefully. Too early, and the route can be unpleasantly icy and the conditions harshly cold. Of course, when having to cross snow bridges, this can be a good thing. This unpleasant cold may have to be tolerated in order to complete part of or all of a journey before a more significant issue arises in early afternoon.

By early afternoon the snow will become impossibly soft underfoot; travel will become difficult; the avalanche risk will sharply rise once again; and it's better to be off the hill. With increased solar heating at this time of year moisture boils up into the atmosphere increasing the chance of afternoon cloud and thunderstorms.

9.7 Spring into summer – perennial snow patches, firns, névés and glaciers

As the temperatures and intensity of solar heating increases with the onset of summer only the deepest most persistent patches of snow remain. These old hard ribbons of snow may be unlikely to avalanche, but they could present a considerable hazard if they need to be crossed. Avoiding a slide on this type of terrain is always better than stopping one. Sensible route choice and the application of step cutting/kicking will help to ensure a safe passage across or round these obstacles.

Of course, there are snow patches of the world that never truly melt back (not yet at least). These are the firn snows or névés of the world's mountains. There are also some fairly benign sections of glacier that form a part of standard trekking routes – mostly on account of the fact that the glacier is receding, and it is a long time since there was any real risk of crevasses opening up. Unless you are absolutely certain that a snow covered glacier is benign, you should always suspect the risk of crevasses, and take the appropriate course of action. Skills for dealing with this type of terrain go beyond the scope of this book. Suffice to say that along with a range of well practiced skills, judgment borne out of experience is a key factor in making good decisions when crossing glaciers.

FIGURE 9.15   CROSSING OLD SNOW IN LATE MAY ON WAY TO GLACIER BLANC HUT IN THE ECRIN   Photo: Mike Rosser

9.7.1 Snow and avalanche
At this time of year, any remaining snow will be the remnants of substantial drifts and patches. Old avalanche debris may remain in the valley bottoms and old ribbons of snow may present an obstacle to the trekker crossing a gully or stream bed.

9.7.2 Snow pack
These patches of seasonal snow are likely to have been through the melt freeze process so often by now that there is very little chance of them avalanching. Having morphed, melted, draped and drooped into their underlying rocks and boulders, these patches are likely to be relatively homogenous, and well anchored to the ground.

9.7.3 Trigger
You would need a stick of dynamite to shift this type of snow, however it is possible that a rapid thaw may lubricate an underlying surface sufficiently that these features may collapse or slide. In this case it is likely to be such severe weather that we are unlikely to be present.

9.7.4 Terrain
These old hard patches of snow are a product of the terrain that caused such deep and stubborn drifts in the first place. Old avalanche trails leave huge deposition cones which may block trekking routes for a long time after the winter has passed. Deep gullies and ravines may cut across a

mountain trail – rendering a simple path into a significant hazard.

9.7.5 Looking after the team
The key problems in the spring are caused by sliding on old snow patches and melt water features known as moulins on dry glaciers.

Avoiding a slide is better than stopping one, and with snow this firm a slide is possible even on easy angled slopes. The consequences of tripping over can also be slightly more serious given the hard landing surface. Thankfully, the firm snow can be readily fashioned into a line of steps, or a good track providing a more secure base for people to walk on. Sturdy winter boots and an ice axe can be a sensible addition, while carrying crampons for a short snow patch crossing may feel over the top. The skills for moving on snow, step cutting with an axe, and even providing security with a rope are important for dealing with this type of terrain. If steps must be cut then other party members should have a ski pole/stick for balance. Consider holding the hand or using a very short rope to give less confident members confidence (see *Figure 9.16*).

For a party leader it is important to consider carefully how groups are to be managed across this type of terrain. Good footwear and an ice axe, if used effectively, will allow all manner of different types of track to be created. This will provide clients with more secure foot placements and reduce the risk of a slip or slide.

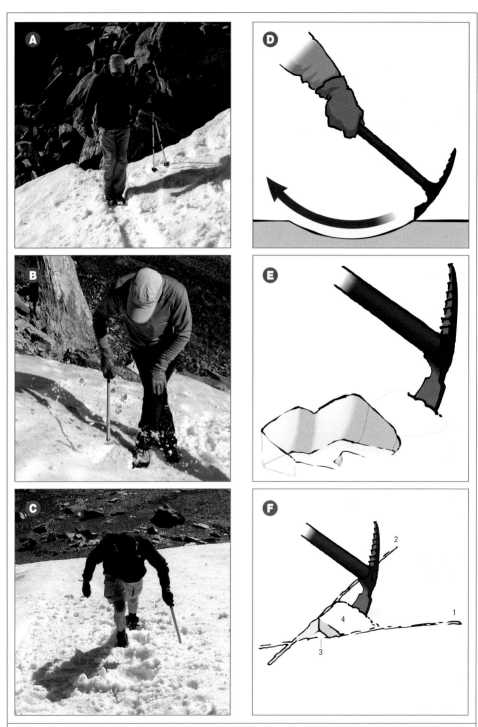

FIGURE 9.16 **A**, **B**, **C** VARIOUS TYPES OF STEPS, TRACKS, CUTTING AND KICKING STEPS **D** A SLASH STEP BEING CUT USING A PENDULUM ACTION WITH THE AXE **E** CUTTING A SIDE STEP: AFTER THE FIRST CUT, EACH SUBSEQUENT BLOW CUTS INTO THE EXISTING HOLE **F** CUTTING A SLAB STEP: THE PICK MAKES THE INITIAL CUTS AND THE AXE IS USED TO REMOVE THE SNOW BETWEEN THEM

Photos: www.pyb.co.uk

Snowshoeing

Photo: Caroline Hale

Movement in the depths of winter can become impossible on foot due to the substantial depths of unconsolidated snow in some parts. The effort required breaking trail through waist-deep snow quickly becomes unsustainable. Therefore snowshoes, or skis, become essential for making progress. Where the snow is hard or ice exists, effective use of crampons is more appropriate.

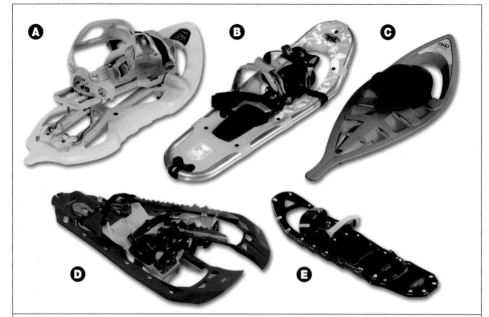

FIGURE 10.01   A VARIETY OF DIFFERENT TYPES OF DESIGNS.   **A** GENERAL PURPOSE SNOW SHOE.   **B** BASIC FRAME AND DECK DESIGN.   **C** BASIC SIMPLE SNOW SHOE DESIGN.   **D** ALL TERRAIN SNOW SHOE WITH CRAMPON POINTS AND SERRATED RIDGES FOR ADDED GRIP.   **E** FRAME AND DECK DESIGN WITH EXTENSION PLATE FOR ADDED FLOTATION.

Snowshoeing is one of the oldest forms of transportation around; historians have traced the origin of snowshoes to Asia sometime between 4,000 and 6,000 BC. For centuries they have allowed people to travel efficiently across snow-covered terrain without sinking. While there are a handful of techniques that will help for more effective use, the saying 'If you can walk, you can snowshoe' is very true.

FIGURE 10.02   A RUNNING STYLE SNOW SHOE MADE FOR RACING, THEIR SHAPE IS DESIGNED TO ALLOW FOR A NATURAL STRIDE.

10.1 Snowshoe design

Historically differences in snowshoe design were likely adaptations to the type of terrain. Even with modern materials, manufacturing and design this is still very much the case today. All snowshoe designs will allow travel across the snow without struggling, but special adaptations to snowshoes make some designs better than others. Three general categories encompass the different types of snowshoe available.

- **Recreational:** these are basic snowshoes for walking on low angle non-rugged terrain and are well suited to walking on established trails. They are good for beginners and are often the type rented from hire facilities in popular Alpine areas.
- **Mountaineering:** this type of snowshoe is more suited to steeper, rugged terrain where traction and durability is important. Some of the differences compared to recreational snow-

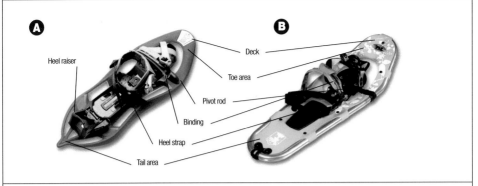

FIGURE 10.03 TWO BASIC STYLES OF SNOW SHOE: **A** COMPOSITE SNOWSHOE. **B** FRAME AND DECK SNOWSHOE.

FIGURE 10.04 TRADITIONAL SNOWSHOE DESIGN
Photo: www.pyb.co.uk

Wearing the right footwear needs careful consideration. Most designs will accommodate a range of different types of footwear from light-weight walking boots to heavier mountainering boots. If you have to make progress without the snowshoes your boots will need to be stiff enough to hold an edge, supportive and warm enough to cope with the conditions.

10.2 Frames and decks

The outer edge of a snowshoe, to which the deck and binding are attached, is considered to be the frame. The decking is the flat surface of the snowshoe that enables you to walk on snow without sinking. While some manufacturers still offer traditional wooden frame snowshoes, most modern designs are made from aluminium or plastic materials, with a synthetic decking used in some cases. Those made from traditional materials such as wood, webbing and canvas are ideal for observing more wildlife, as they are 'quiet' to walk in as opposed to those made from plastic which tend to be a little noisier. An alternative to the frame and deck design uses a one-piece plastic moulded deck onto which the binding is mounted. Both styles work well but the latter provides more options for adding extras to allow for different types of terrain and conditions *(see Figure 10.03)*.

shoes may be noticeable, like larger teeth on the cleats or a little more weight to the snowshoe; but the real difference is often in stronger frames, bindings, and the myriad of little parts that hold a snowshoe together.

- ***Running:*** these snowshoes are designed for cross-training and competitive racing. They are about two-thirds the weight of snowshoes in the above categories, and offer less flotation, but optimal agility for the niche sport of running or racing on trails covered with packed (usually groomed) snow *(see Figure 10.02)*.

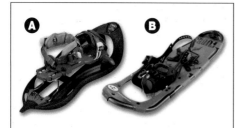

FIGURE 10.05 **PIVOT BINDINGS** ALLOW THE SNOW-
SHOE TO PIVOT AND THE TAIL TO DROP AS YOU WALK,
LETTING SNOW SLIDE OFF AND ALLOWING FOR EASIER
CLIMBING. **FIXED BINDINGS** DON'T PIVOT VERY MUCH
AND KEEP THE HEELS LEVEL WITH EACH STEP, MAKING
FOR A MORE NATURAL STRIDE ON FLAT TERRAIN
AND MAKING IT POSSIBLE TO WALK BACKWARDS.
A PIVOT BINDING. **B** FIXED BINDING.

10.3 Bindings

Bindings are used to secure boots to snowshoes
and usually consist of a platform and nylon
straps that go over the foot and around the heel.
When choosing snowshoes it is important to
make sure they are compatible with your footwear and that the binding system is easy to use
especially with gloves on *(see Figure 10.05)*.

Bindings are either **pivoting** or **fixed**. Pivoting
bindings allow for a more natural gait and an
easier time climbing hills or kicking steps. Fixed
bindings don't pivot very much, but make it
easier to reverse or step over obstacles, since the

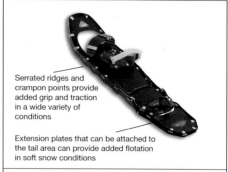

Serrated ridges and
crampon points provide
added grip and traction
in a wide variety of
conditions

Extension plates that can be attached to
the tail area can provide added flotation
in soft snow conditions

FIGURE 10.06   TRACTION AND TAIL EXTENSIONS

snowshoe's tail doesn't flop around. Most
bindings will work with a wide variety of footwear. However some are designed specifically
for larger mountaineering or ski boots, or to
snugly fit running shoes. So make sure the
bindings will work with any preferred footwear.

10.4 Traction devices

Although your weight provides some traction by
pushing the snowshoes into the snow, many
designs feature tooth-like crampons or cleats for
greater grip. Recreational-style snowshoes will
typically offer moderate amounts of traction,
while mountaineering snowshoes will generally

FIGURE 10.07   COL DE COU, SWISS-FRENCH BORDER

Photo: Caroline Hale

have more aggressive crampons and cleats for steep rugged ground and icy conditions.

- **Toe** or **instep crampons** are located on the undersides of the bindings, so they pivot with your feet and dig into the snow as you climb. This is the primary source of traction for any snowshoe.
- **Heel crampons** are placed on the decking undersides of many snowshoes. They are frequently in a V formation, which fills with snow and slows you down on descent.
- **Side rails** on the decking undersides provide lateral stability and reduce side-slipping when traversing slopes.
- **Braking bars** are integrated into the undersides of plastic-decking snowshoes to provide forward traction and prevent sliding backwards.

10.5 Heel raisers

Also known as **climbing bars**, these wire or plastic bails can be flipped up under the heels to relieve calf strain on steep uphill sections and save energy on long ascents *(see Figure 10.08)*.

10.6 Snowshoe size

Correctly sizing snowshoes for a person is largely determined by the approximate weight that will be placed. This should not only take account of body weight but any extra equipment they may carry. For example if they are travelling with a heavy rucksack on expedition they will probably require a larger snowshoe compared to normal. In general, the heavier the person or load, the bigger the snowshoe will need to be to disperse the weight in order to keep that person on top of the snow. Snowshoe size is also partially determined by terrain and snow conditions. For example, larger shoes are required to keep a person afloat in light powder snow than are necessary in wet, packed or icy snow. Some designs offer the flexibility to add an extra section to the tail increasing the amount of float. As a rule of thumb, use the smallest size that will support your weight for the snow conditions and terrain. As long as there is adequate flotation, smaller snowshoes will be much easier to handle and manoeuvre. To assist with sizing manufacturers often design models for different weight

FIGURE 10.08   USING HEEL LIFTERS ON MODERATE GRADIENTS HELPS TO KEEP THE FOOT LEVEL WHEN WALKING IN SNOW SHOES UPHILL. THIS CAN IMPROVE STABILITY AND BALANCE WHILE REDUCING STRESS ON THE LOWER LEG.

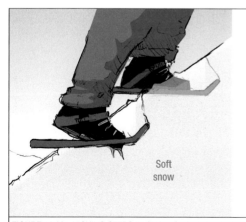

Soft snow

Hard snow

FIGURE 10.09   KICKING STEPS IN SNOW SHOES ON SHORT STEEP SLOPES

FIGURE 10.10 SIDE-STEPPING, SIDE-KICKING AND HERRINGBONE STEPPING

10.7 Snowshoeing techniques – going up

When walking up gently sloping terrain it is easiest to climb directly up the hill facing forward. As the slope increases in grade or the soft snow depth increases it will then become easier to traverse at a suitable angle to the slope. Short zigzags for steep and narrow slopes and longer ones on wider expanses will help to maintain a steady angle upwards and avoid traversing straight across the fall line of the slope. Snowshoes tend not to work well when traversing, especially in hard snow conditions. On narrow trails or paths sometimes the only option is to ascend straight up. This requires some practice and technique and can be difficult in soft snow. Use care to try and maintain the new track for following snowshoers.

- In powdery snow a **kick-step** offers the best method for secure ascent of slopes. By kicking into the snow with the toe of the boot to create a step and trying to keep your heels level it will plant the crampons or cleats into the snow, directly under the balls of your feet, so as to gain maximum traction. The snowshoes will be on the angle of the slope, with the tails hanging downhill behind. If conditions are such that a kick-step ends up creating a deep hole in the snow, then look for a different route.

- On crusty, hard pack snow or icy surfaces, it may not be possible to kick a step. The traction devices on the underside of the snowshoe play more of a role in these situations, and good positive footwork is still important to ensure they are pushed into the snow to gain security. If walking directly up a slope in these conditions is difficult consider zigzagging or choosing an alternative route.

- On moderate to steep slopes, flip up the **heel raisers** feature under the heel, as this puts your legs in a more comfortable position for long ascents *(see Figure 10.08).*

Other techniques for ascending may include sidestepping, side-kicking and herringbone stepping *(see Figure 10.10).*

ranges and provide charts accordingly. Many also produce snowshoes specifically designed for men, women and children.

The basic shape of a snowshoe will affect its ability to handle in different terrain and types of snow. For example a snowshoe with a long toe and short tail struggles in deep soft snow or crust with the toe often catching under the surface requiring it to be pulled free to prevent a fall. Wider snowshoes will work well in deep powder and more shaped decks will allow for easier walking and a more natural gait *(see Figure 10.03).*

FIGURE 10.11 DESCENDING

Photo: Carlo Forte

10.8 Snowshoeing techniques – going down

Descents can often provide the most fun in a day out on snowshoes. Good dynamic body position and balance allow for ease of movement and the ability to react as the ground changes so as to avoid falling over. When using poles keep them planted in front of you with knees bent and relaxed and your body weight slightly back. Walk smoothly and plant heel first, then toe. It will help to consider the following.

- The instinct will be to lean back on the snowshoe tails. This reaction works well on models with angled crampons built into the heel, which are designed to dig in as you descend.
- When wearing snowshoes without heel crampons, you'll need to keep your weight over your feet, so your toe crampons will be planted firmly. Poles will provide a great deal more balance and control as you descend.
- Commit down the fall line when walking downhill; shying away from the slope will reduce your grip, make you more likely to slide, and reduce your chances of staying on top of the shoes if they do slide a little. Keep your weight forward and keep your 'nose over your toes'.
- Consider others who may ascend using your tracks. Try to avoid damaging the track you have left and if possible pick a path of fresh snow away from your ascending trail. In busy areas other snowshoe parties will be very grateful.

Many snowshoes have the facility to lock the heel down and this is a particularly useful feature when descending in soft snow. Performing any complex manoeuvres or reversing is made much easier with heels locked in place *(see Figure 10.11)*.

FIGURE 10.12   SKI POLES IN ACTION   Photo: Caroline Hale

FIGURE 10.13   TRAVERSING

FIGURE 10.14   A USEFUL WAY OF USING POLES TO PUSH ON TO HELP STAND UP AND REGAIN BALANCE

10.9 Traversing

Traversing a slope is often used when trying to avoid overly steep or difficult terrain. Keeping your balance is key. When traversing, depending on your type of snowshoe, let the ankle flex to give you maximum contact with the snow. In some conditions it may be necessary to edge on a traverse, but this will put strain on both your lower body and the snowshoes. Increased torsion on the front binding may cause failure *(see Figure 10.13)*.

10.10 Ski poles

Poles are perhaps optional on flat terrain, but on most snowshoeing trips they almost become essential. They provide support while stepping up or down and with manoeuvrability and balance. Adjustable poles are best. They can be shortened for uphill travel, lengthened for descending, and when crossing slopes, one can be extended for the downhill side and the other shortened for the uphill side. Pole length should be adjusted so your arm is bent at a right angle *(see Figure 10.12)*.

FIGURE 10.15 TRACK BEING MADE BY A GROUP   Photo: www.pyb.co.uk

10.11 Getting yourself back up

To get back up from a fall can take a lot of effort, particularly if the snow is soft and deep or if you have a large rucksack. Using your poles can help to minimise the effort required *(see Figure 10.14)*.

10.12 Repair kits

While modern snowshoes are designed for function and the potential abuse they might receive, things do break from time to time. This is especially the case if they are used in terrain beyond which they are intended for. As an example recreational snowshoes may struggle with the demands of more rugged terrain. Failure of the snowshoe can cause a problem at any time; however in more remote places it could potentially jeopardise any further travel. Carrying a few spares and some extra bits and pieces could allow for a temporary repair to be made *(see **Appendix II Repair kit** on page 171)*.

10.13 Track setting skills

Good track setting is a subtle yet rewarding art. The aim is to achieve the right balance between a direct route to your objective, with a consistent rate of ascent in an effortless series of switch-backs and rolls which make use of natural terrain features. But there is more to a good track than physically making progress; consider where the track goes, what the risks are, and what threat there may be from above you.

FIGURE 10.16 DIGGING SNOW HOLES FOR SHELTER IN A WIND SCOOP   Photo: www.pyb.co.uk

Use the CRAFT acronym – route setting is a **CRAFT**. Consider the **R**oute overall; try to set a consistent **A**ngle or rate of ascent; make use of natural **F**eatures; and consider the **T**errain or threats from above you.

When setting a track, try to be constantly mindful of three degrees of scale.

- The final objective
- The next obstacle or feature to negotiate
- The immediate conditions underfoot (and the resulting quality of the track)

Try to consider all three of these at the same time or at least in rapid succession. This will allow you to keep to the shortest overall route, while looking ahead to encounter any features in your path *(see Figure 10.15)*.

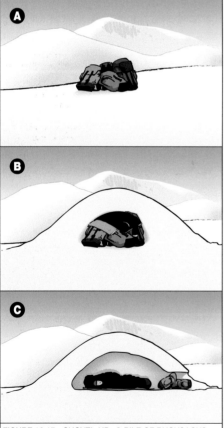

FIGURE 10.17   SHOVEL-UP: **A** PILE OF RUCKSACKS TO PILE SNOW ON FOR SHOVEL-UP **B** COVER SACKS WITH FABRIC, SUCH AS OUTER SHELL, AND COMPACT SNOW ON TOP **C** DIG OUT PACKS FROM THE SIDE TO MAKE AN ENTRANCE AND ENLARGE INTERIOR TO SUIT

When snowshoeing in a group it is most effective to share trail breaking duties. Swap leads every few minutes depending on the depth of soft snow and the nature of the terrain. Taking turns will allow the entire party to move faster over the ground.

12.14 Snow shelters

The decision to spend a night or any significant length of time out in 'winter conditions' should never be taken lightly. Every effort should be made to get to a safer more sheltered area, even if this means a lengthy walk. There may well be a few situations where the decision is obvious: exhaustion, injury, hypothermia or lost in severe weather in a region of serious ground.

If caught out by unforeseen circumstances the ability to make some sort of emergency shelter could be of paramount importance. In early season with very little available snow making a satisfactory shelter can be a difficult task. The answer is to be creative with what you are carrying and can muster together. Group equipment such as group shelters, trekking poles and rucksacks can all be usefully employed. Likewise, time looking for natural features such as tree wells, boulders, nooks and crannies that may be improved upon to provide shelter is often time well spent. A good snow shovel allows for all manner of jobs to be done quickly and efficiently from shovelling snow for shelter building to digging steps or tracks through the snow. In winter conditions they should be considered an essential part of your equipment.

10.15 The shovel-up

The 'shovel-up' or 'quinzhee' is a versatile shelter, relatively easy to construct and can be built almost anywhere. It has several major advantages over other types of snow shelters allowing it to be built in flat safe places, away from avalanche risk and where there is insufficient depth of snow for other types of shelter. On the downside it can become vulnerable rather quickly in a thaw.

Somewhere naturally sheltered that can be exploited is often worth seeking out and will save time in construction. Shovelling snow downhill with gravity is easier than shovelling uphill. Therefore building a shelter in a hollow surrounded by higher ground, against a bank, or at the base of a slope can save time *(see Figure 10.19)*.

To construct this type of shelter, a mound of snow is piled up and then hollowed out. The act of moving and piling the snow produces changes in it so that it rapidly consolidates. To make both shovelling up and hollowing out easier, a pile of rucksacks or similar can be the starting point for the mound the size of which will depend on the number of people it must hold. Covering the rucksacks and equipment with a bivi bag or group shelter will help when trying to hollow out. To begin with mark out a circle in the snow approximately a metre radius more than the internal size required. Lay the rucksacks in this and pile snow on top, patting down regularly. When the mound is large enough to hollow out and leave walls about 0.3 to 0.5 metres thick, begin burrowing in on the lee side to retrieve the sacks. Inserting sticks from the outside will give a measure of how thick the walls are. It should now be possible to start hollowing out the mound from the inside until it is large enough. You can also continue carefully to pile the already disturbed snow from the inside of the shelter onto the roof to increase the mound size. Once complete rucksacks, branches and blocks

of snow can be used to shelter or block the entrance. Be careful not to seal the doorway too well especially if cooking inside the shelter as this will reduce ventilation. Any spare equipment can be used as seats providing some insulation from the ground *(see Figure 10.18)*.

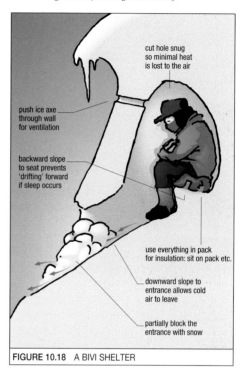

cut hole snug so minimal heat is lost to the air

push ice axe through wall for ventilation

backward slope to seat prevents 'drifting' forward if sleep occurs

use everything in pack for insulation: sit on pack etc.

downward slope to entrance allows cold air to leave

partially block the entrance with snow

FIGURE 10.18 A BIVI SHELTER

FIGURE 10.19 A SHOVEL-UP

Photo: www.pyb.co.uk

Deep snow – up and over lower branches of tree

Branches stacked against tree if snow not deep enough

Packed snow

Ground

Evergreen boughs

FIGURE 10.20   A 'FIR-TREE SHELTER'

10.16 Other types of shelters

Many other types of shelter can be fashioned although most rely on the presence of deeper snow cover and specific sites. A simple bivi shelter as shown in *Figure 10.18* can be made by digging into a steep bank of snow. Once again using a shovel or axe it is possible to create a small shelter for one person to escape the elements. In a group it can be most efficient if everyone digs their own hole into a bank next to one another so that they may be linked together when complete.

Given the environment that snowshoeing often takes place in, it may be worth mentioning the 'fir tree shelter'. This uses the downward sloping branches at the bottom of a fir tree that holds snow *(see Figure 10.20)*.

Dealing with problems while travelling

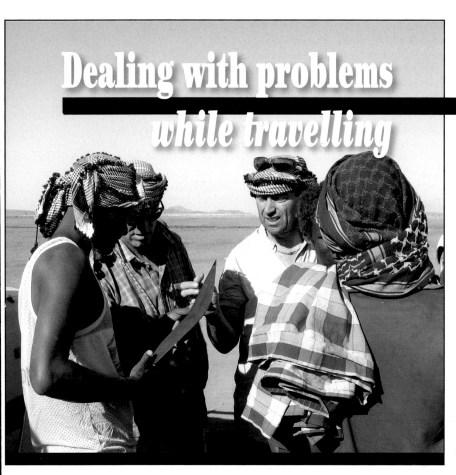

FRIEND OR FOE IN ETHIOPIA

Photo: Iain Peter

To lose documents, be a victim of a crime, become ill, or be involved in an accident in a foreign country is an unpleasant and distressing experience. When these things happen in a remote environment the stress is far greater, the situation is potentially more complex and the possibility of feelings of vulnerability, uncertainty and isolation for individuals involved is significantly increased.

No one likes to look for problems but thinking through potential emergency situations will raise awareness and hopefully avoid problems occurring.

Unfortunately even with the best planning and most cautious approach things can go wrong. Awareness, preparation and planning may not reduce the unpleasantness of the incident but they may ensure that some problems are more easily solved. Developing protocols for certain situations that could befall a group will provide support and some certainty to those involved. By having systems in place it is possible to take some of the pressure out of a situation and also contribute to finding quick solutions.

When beginning to plan a trip invest in a good travel guide and access the Foreign and Commonwealth Office website *(see Figure 11.01)*. This excellent site has up to the minute advice on travel anywhere in the world. It is possible to

register online with the FCO for a service called 'LOCATE'. In the event of a disaster in the region you are visiting the FCO would endeavour to contact you in order to ensure that you are safe and provide advice if required. It would also help your family to contact you if there was a problem here at home.

The FCO will provide information and contact details of embassies, consulates or high commissions in the area you are visiting. It is useful to carry these details with you, as in the event of a serious emergency you are very likely to need their support and advice.

11.1 Documents

Probably the most common incident is the loss of documents, tickets and or money. Before travelling it is a good idea to make copies of all documents including insurance policy numbers and contact details and store them in a different place to the originals. It is also useful to scan documents, essential contact details and phone numbers and store these in a secure location on the internet. Finally it is useful to leave a copy of documents, insurance details and an itinerary with a reliable member of the family or a friend who is available during your time of travel.

11.2 Money

Money should be organised in advance so that you arrive with some local currency. In an ideal world, it is useful to access money in a number of different ways, for example cash, travellers cheques (record the cheque numbers before you go) and credit cards (record the card number and carry the emergency lost and stolen contact telephone numbers appropriate for the country you are visiting). The ease of using credit cards and travellers cheques varies from country to country and place to place so check carefully before you leave. Frequently travellers and local agents are a more reliable and up to date source for this information. Internet banking may offer a secure way of transferring money but requires technology and access to a bank.

(Y) Leader's Information

Serious incident guidance

For those leading groups and working for an organisation there would normally be a 'Serious Incident Guidance Brief' and a 24-hour contact number.

However for those who are working as sole operators it may be an important consideration to organise home backup. In the event of an emergency you may need to access a group member's details urgently or it may even be the leader who has the problem!

FIGURE 11.01   THE FOREIGN AND COMMONWEALTH OFFICE WEB HOMEPAGE

The more remote an area, the more reliant on carrying cash you are likely to be. This may involve changing a large quantity of money. It is always advisable to use a trusted source such as a bank rather than the back of a 'carpet shop' even though you may not get such a good exchange rate. Consider changing money in a number of different venues; it is certainly a good idea not to go alone and to have only the amount of money you wish to change in view. Count the money carefully with the teller and do not leave the office without checking. Similarly when you go to pay for items have just over the required amount in your wallet or purse.

When carrying large amounts of money try to use small denomination notes and consider securely packaging small bundles and stowing them around your body. If in a group, share them around the group and record who is carrying what to avoid confusion.

Where pre-payments can be made to providers by internet payment do this and carry a copy of the evidence of payment.

11.3 Theft

In any country it is possible to find yourself a victim of theft. However with a few simple precautions it is possible not to be a beacon of opportunity by not flaunting items that exemplify wealth such as watches and cameras. Keep money and documents in a discreet body wallet hidden under clothes and keep a sum of ready money easily accessible.

When trekking and camping it is probably a good idea to keep all valuables on you or in the rucksack you are carrying. When in the mountains there is very little need for documents or money therefore packaging valuables in a robust plastic case and sealing with duct tape will protect them from the weather. It is harder to identify what the contents are and makes it easier to hide them in discrete places such as down the back of the rucksack or among dirty clothes! Leaving valuables in an unattended tent or camp is not to be recommended. In parts of Africa, belongings left unattended are deemed to be abandoned!

FIGURE 11.02   CHINESE POLICEMAN IN TIBET   Photo: Iain Peter

FIGURE 11.03   BASE CAMP AT SNOW LAKE, PAKISTAN

Photo: Pete Stacey

 Leader's Information

Money briefing

It is important to brief the members of your group, preferably before departure, so that they can prepare their belongings, travel wallets and money and leave unnecessary valuables at home.

Unfortunately in some areas care also needs to be taken when in a tent. A number of unfortunate victims have found neat holes cut in the fly and inner and wallets removed. Hidden in the bottom of a sleeping bag may be a more secure place.

If you or a member of your group is a victim of theft then you should record everything that has been taken and any other relevant details. If staying in a hotel inform the management immediately and ensure that the police are called and insist on a police report at the earliest opportunity. Credit cards and travellers cheques should be stopped as soon as possible. Ensure you have a list of the appropriate numbers to call. If passports and travel documents have been stolen then the local British Embassy, High Commission or Consulate will have to be contacted. They will be able to issue temporary replacement documents and offer advice and support. If the theft is likely to involve an insurance claim then the insurance company should also be notified at the earliest possible moment.

11.4 Assault and rape

It does not follow that a person is any more likely to be attacked while travelling abroad than at home. As with all countries, cities and towns there are safe places to travel and less safe ones. As a traveller you are only at increased risk because you are a visitor, potentially with greater wealth and less ability to communicate.

In towns and cities there are simple precautions that every one can take; namely to use guide books, hotels, tourist information and agents to discover good local venues to explore and areas to avoid. In public places dress modestly and cover up as this tends to denote a respect for yourself (both men and women) and you will attract less attention. When going out ensure that you have the hotel address, map and telephone number. At night use recommended taxis and avoid getting involved in drinking with strangers. It is obviously safer not to explore alone but for some people that is their pleasure. It is a good idea for the single traveller to leave a note of their itinerary with the hotel and have a regular contact back home.

Leader's Information

Incident procedure

In the event of a member of your group reporting a theft to you or you finding yourself a victim it is important not to ignore the incident but also not to inflame the situation. Firstly listen carefully and do not make promises you cannot enforce. Possibly the best course of action is to calmly inform every one of what has taken place and what your actions will be. This is just to remind everyone to be more vigilant with their belongings; this will also inform the potential perpetrator that the loss has not gone unnoticed. Never make an unfounded accusation and be cautious of any accusation where you have no back up. Remember in areas where tourism is very important to the local economy, locals may have very harsh penalties for members of their community being seen putting their reputation at risk, therefore an inaccurate allegation could be very damaging.

11.5 Accidents and injury

Travelling and trekking in the remote areas of the world is an exhilarating, interesting and fulfilling experience. Accidents can happen anywhere and when things go wrong in a remote environment decisions will need to be made about short and long term care of both the casualty and group. A worthwhile investment for any leader or independent trekker would be training in 'remote medicine' or 'wilderness care' plus a pocket sized medical care book. A combination of training and a well planned medical kit appropriate to the area is essential to every traveller *(see **Chapter 4 Staying healthy** on page 37)*. A leader should ensure that they are adequately trained and familiar with the contents of the medical kit.

In the event of a serious incident the ability to call for help, raise a rescue team or simply to talk to a calm voice for reassurance can be invaluable. Following a traumatic event it is generally acknowledged that most survivors need to be rescued within the first 24 hours – 'The Golden day'.

 Leader's Information

Staying together

As a leader of a group it is very important to brief members well, to encourage individuals to consider going out in groups and to leave an itinerary of their day as well as ensuring that they have contact details for you and the hotel.

When camping on a trek it is useful to camp close to others and on officially designated sites or, if in a more remote location, to try and camp in a discreet spot and not draw attention to the location by lighting fires.

Photo: Iain Peter

11.6 Communication

The communications world has changed dramatically offering a number of choices.

11.6.1. Mobile/cell phones

Mobile phones will work in a surprising number of coun-tries. In vast countries such as South America and China aerials are far easier to erect and maintain than cables. It is possible to be sleeping in a mud hut in a remote village and still have mobile phone reception. Before travelling it is important to contact your phone provider to check whether your contract will allow calls and or texts to be made in the area. Not all types of phone work worldwide so it is important to ensure that a cellular phone has the capacity to work in the area being visited. Taking an unlocked phone and then purchasing an in-country SIM card can be a useful solution.

Problems at camp

When organising a camping group it may be appropriate to place male tents in one area, female in another and mixed between them. The down side of segregating areas is that an intruder can easily locate all female tents in one area. Therefore if the group are known to each other and the leader then it may offer some security by mixing the tents randomly. A leader may wish the privacy of locating their tent away from the group. If supervising groups of young people, however, it is important for the leader to be close enough to be easily disturbed by a problem or unusual activity in the night, while not over-stepping the appropriate protocols of child protection.

A time when all individuals wish for privacy is when going to the toilet. However in certain locations at night it may be appropriate to ask young people to go to the toilet in pairs or to tell a companion where they are going.

If a member of your group is unfortunate enough to become a victim of an assault or rape it is important to listen and be non-judgemental. It may be appropriate to include in the conversation a friend or relative of the victim to give support. In some countries attitudes to sexual crime may be very different and therefore it may be helpful to contact the nearest Embassy, High Commission or Consulate and seek their advice about procedures. This should all be done as quickly as possible if the crime is to be investigated and remember that evidence will be lost should the victim wash or change.

If the incident happens in a remote location ensure that an account of what happened is recorded, if appropriate include photographs. Once again inform the police and ensure that the Embassy is are informed at the earliest possible opportunity.

Photo: Mike Rosser

11.6.2. Satellite phones

In remote locations where terrestrial cells phones (mobile phone) may not work, satellite phones can now provide near worldwide coverage *(see Figure 11.04)*.

Geosynchronous services are able to maintain a near worldwide coverage using a small number of satellites at a very high altitude. These systems are capable of providing enough band width to provide internet services. However, the disadvantages are a delay in transmitting time when making a call and that signal can be blocked by mountains, steep ground and even forests. Users should note that in some countries the use of a sat-phone is illegal without a licence e.g. India.

11.6.3. Low earth orbit telephones

LEO systems use a greater number of satellites orbiting the world at lower altitudes. They pro-vide worldwide coverage and are less susceptible to signal blockage as the satellites are moving so if one is blocked another will quickly come into range.

As in all phone technology satellite phones have continued to decrease in size and increase in use. Unfortunately it is also true to say that the better the technology the more expensive the phone. Satellite phones are purpose built for the provider network and therefore it is not possible to switch between networks. Investing in a satellite phone is a significant cost but fortunately there are a number of companies that specialise in satellite phone rental. They are able to provide advice, phones and temporary contracts at a fraction of the cost of purchase. The service is generally very efficient but requires forethought as documentation needs to be exchanged and equipment dispatched. At present

FIGURE 11.04   USING A SAT PHONE IN ALASKA   Photo: Iain Peter

Iridium is recognised as having the best world-wide coverage.

If travelling for extended periods of time into remote locations then extra batteries will need to be carried or the ability to use a solar charger might be considered.

Calling costs, both to and from satellite phones, are generally quite high. On an organised trip some of the cost of the phone rental may be recouped by charging clients extra for calls. In remote cold locations it may be very difficult to maintain battery charge and therefore the use of the phone may need to be kept to emergency use only. Before travelling it is important to inform people, both those on the trip and those at home of the cost of calls, availability of the satellite phone and whether it will be possible to receive incoming calls.

The benefit of a phone is that it can be used for communication convenience as well as in the event of an emergency. In an emergency a phone has the benefit that a clear picture of the incident can be communicated and support can be offered from a base. The down side is that it requires someone with knowledge to be on the other end of the phone and for a member of the party to be able to use the phone.

It should be noted that any emergency plans must take into account that there may be times that neither mobile nor satellite phone have a signal.

11.6.4. Distress radio beacons

These devices are tracking transmitters that aid in the rescue and location boats (EPIRB), aircraft (ELT) and people (PLB) in remote locations away from the normal emergency and rescue services *(see Figure 11.06)*.

Personal locator beacons (PLB) are relatively small, robust devices that are capable of transmitting a distress message that will alert the nearest search and rescue organisation. From February 2009 only beacons transmitting on digital 406 MHz are detected by satellites therefore older beacons transmitting on other frequencies are obsolete. In analogue mode beacons transmit 121.5MHz which can be picked up by aircraft. This signal will be emitted continuously until the battery dies. PLBs can be sold either with or without GPS. The benefit of GPS is that the operation becomes a rescue as opposed to a search and rescue.

Every PLB is sold with a unique Hex code which identifies the owner. PLBs should be registered with the appropriate home national

FIGURE 11.06   SPOT BEACON

FIGURE 11.07   SIMPLE TWO-WAY RADIOS

authority. In the event of an incident this would give the relevant Search and Rescue Body phone contact details, a description of the person or group plus details of the home base. Therefore it is important to consider what information and whose contact details should be given. In the event of a beacon being detected the contact information will be used to verify the problem, so it is essential that a knowledgeable person is familiar with the group's itinerary and activities. About 97 per cent of all alerts are false but with registered beacons 70 per cent of false alerts can be resolved saving on a potentially very costly and unnecessary rescue and even fines.

Again the cost of beacons varies dramatically but you get what you pay for. A GPS-based registered beacon might cost £1000 but they can send a location to within 100m, send the serial information and have the next of kin contacted within four minutes.

The benefit of a beacon is that a rescue can be mobilised very quickly. However, without other means of communication there is no ability for the group involved to pass on or receive information.

11.6.5. Radios

Small two-way radios are now available at every airport electrical shop. They are limited in their use by range and physical land features but they can be an invaluable tool when dealing with a number of groups. They are usually only 'line of sight' and generally limited to a range of 2-4km. Other than the purchase price and batteries communication between units is free (see Figure 11.07).

11.7 Rescue

In the event of an emergency having a plan is often the key to a successful outcome. The situation becomes more difficult to deal with when in a more remote or alien environment. Problems with conditions, terrain and communication can all mean the process of concluding an incident takes considerably longer. Prior to departure on any trip it is always worth spending time thinking about how to deal with an emergency at different stages of the journey. In much the same way as conducting a risk assessment, considering what may go wrong at certain stages and how it might get solved beforehand is always time well spent. The European Alps are well catered for in terms of search and rescue facilities. Most countries throughout this region have highly skilled professional organisations conducting all manner of mountain rescue operations. These are often private organisations that charge for the service and because most use helicopters as their primary tool for search and rescue the costs can be high. Therefore, it is important to have the necessary insurance to cover for these eventualities (see **Chapter 2 Insurance** on page 11). In less developed countries and especially in more remote wilderness areas rescue may not be as straightforward. Some countries, as in the UK, rely on volunteers and charitable organisations for rescue facilities, as well as the RAF. In other countries it may be the responsibility of the military to deal with such situations. Either way it could be more complex and requires some research beforehand. Spend time researching the search and rescue cover for the chosen location. It is paramount to establish contact details for these organisations so that they may be informed as to the nature of any emergency with minimum delay. Even with a sophisticated system in place communication can be difficult, particularly if there is a language barrier. By minimising the chain of calls it will reduce the potential for any distortion in the information given and therefore increase the chances of a successful outcome. The planning stage could be a good opportunity to consider these issues and produce a 'master plan', which can be used in the event of such situations. An emergency procedure plan will take the pressure off having to make decisions on the spot. This plan should be documented and travel with you so that it may be used in the field as reference. It is very difficult to produce a plan for every eventuality, as each incident is unique; however a generic plan will provide support for most situations. Contact numbers for emergency services and in-country agencies should be included as well as the details of embassies and insurers.

Depending on the country or countries visited the rescue facilities may be very limited. In remote regions rescue may take several days or longer if the conditions are poor *(see Figure 11.08)*. Having the appropriate equipment to deal with a possible situation becomes more of a consideration the more remote a trip becomes. Effective communication is fundamental to obtaining help and while a sat-phone may seem like a 'get out jail free card' if it refuses to work there needs to be some contingency. This may include sending for help in some way or having a plan in place with an agency/embassy that can be initiated in the event of a missed rendezvous *(see **Communication, EPIRBs** on page 158)*.

Many countries will use planes and helicopters to search for people requiring assistance. In some countries you may be required to put down a rescue or helicopter bond which could be in excess of a $1000 dollars. Some agencies will accept insurance documents but others will require cash; this is refundable on your return unless you have used it!

In remote regions the rescue services may need to cover considerable distances to reach a location before conducting a search. For this reason is becomes important to make yourself as visible as possible when in need of help. Build a fire, or lay brightly coloured clothing or material on a dark surface to attract attention. By night a torch can be used or flares if they are available. If 'buzzed' by an aircraft the international distress signal of raising your hands above your head in a 'Y' shape will signal to the pilot that you require help *(see Figure 11.10)*.

Considering the emergency procedures for any particular trip is an important part of the planning stage. Involving everyone in the creation of this plan will encourage conversation and debate about such issues, giving team members a greater understanding of the procedures and how to implement them. The detail and content of any plan will vary according to the type of trip, the available rescue services, the equipment carried and the nature of the group. However, any plan should allow the leader or team members to initiate a process by which the following can occur.

- Immediate care of the casualty(s) and group
- Evacuation of casualty(s) to relevant medical care
- Possible evacuation of group or change to itinerary
- Revision of expedition plans
- Communicating with base/employer/school/company/home
- Monitoring of casualty(s) care
- Contacting local agencies/embassies for support
- Contacting family or relatives
- Contacting insurance company

FIGURE 11.08 HELICOPTER RESCUE
Photo: John Cousins

FIGURE 11.09   TRANSPORT ON THE TIBETAN PLATEUX   Photo: Mal Creasey

Need help?

Yes   No

FIGURE 11.10   THE INTERNATIONAL DISTRESS SIGNAL
FOR **YES** AND **NO**

Having a plan will help when faced with tricky
decisions such as who do I send for help? Can we
help ourselves? How long can we stay in the
same place? Remember, it is important all team
members are informed about these plans as it
may be you that requires assistance. Indeed this
is a good motivation for making sure a system is
in place.

11.8 Minor accidents and injuries

As a trek leader if a member of your group is
involved in a minor accident or has a small injury,
the incident and injury should always be treated
and recorded. Any injury, no matter how innocu-
ous, should be monitored as neglect may easily
lead to further problems. As an example the best
solution for a blister is avoidance but should a
blister occur it needs to be kept clean and well
padded. Should an infection set in then the
person may at best be unable to walk and at
worse may become very ill. Combine this with
being ten days out on a remote trek and you now
have a serious problem.

11.9 Serious incident and major accident

In the event of a serious accident the priority for
any leader is first their own safety and second the
safety of the rest of the group. This is especially
important in a remote setting. Once it is estab-

lished that the situation is stable then the needs of the injured person can be dealt with.

It is generally recognised that giving people tasks and keeping them informed is very important in helping them deal with an incident. It is important to have an overview of the incident and delegate where appropriate. Decisions will need to be made as to what assistance is required if available, how long will it take the casualty to be evacuated or managed by the group. Some organisations have access to doctors who can talk and advise via sat-phone to leaders dealing with either a medical emergency or accident.

Long term care for a seriously injured casualty in a remote location is vital and consideration will need to be made with regards pain management and infection control. This obviously goes beyond the training provided by a standard first aid course. If working for an organisation they should be contacted as soon as possible as the media may well take an interest in the event. When convenient, the insurance company will also need to be informed as to the nature of the incident. They may be able to offer advice and assistance but if the situation is under control the insurance company will also need to be continually updated, especially when considering repatriation.

As soon as possible a record should be kept of the incident and all actions that followed. Group members should be asked to write their own account and they should be given the opportunity to talk about what happened both as a group and individuals. Opportunities should be offered in different ways and at different times. Once the event has past it is very important that there is some closure and that everyone is informed of the outcome, whether it is good or bad. Knowledge is better than uncertainty.

It is useful for people to understand that a traumatic event may affect them in different ways both in the present and the future. There is no prescribed correct reaction; some people will apparently not be affected, others may have highly emotional responses and possibly flashbacks. All reactions in the period following an event are apparently normal. A reaction to a traumatic event can become a more serious problem when it starts to have an effect on everyday life. In this case the individual may be suffering from post traumatic stress and may need to seek professional help and counselling.

11.10 Fatalities

If a death occurs in a town or city then the procedure is relatively straightforward as long as it is not a suspicious death. A doctor will need to be called and the police may need to be informed. The insurance company will need to be informed as next of kin may wish to travel to the location and the body will need repatriating. The death should be registered in the country where the person died for which all relevant documentation will be required. The death does not need to be registered with the FCO but they are always a good source of support and they may be able to issue a UK death certificate.

If a fatality occurs in a remote location the formalities are all delayed and it may be impossible for a doctor to travel to the location. In this event whether the death is due to an accident or apparent natural causes it is important to record as much information as possible, including taking photographs. It is important to include everyone in detailing your actions so they are understood. Record what happened prior to the death as well as after and ask group members to do the same. If possible send for medical assistance and the police as well as contacting any home support and the insurance company. It is very important to be discreet as it may attract media attention.

If the body has to be moved or the whole party has to remain in one place for a time it is important that the body is treated with respect and disturbed as little as possible. If it is possible it should be kept cool, covered and protected.

Even with access to a satellite phone it is not appropriate to be informing next of kin of a death and that duty would normally fall to the FCO consular staff or the police.

Following a serious incident on a trek people may have different opinions as to whether they wish to go on or go home. It is best not to assume but to sit and discuss the options and allow people to make their own decisions.

11.11 Injury to a leader

It is not beyond the realms of possibility that a leader may be badly injured or taken very ill. All leaders should carry an information pack and incident check list to cover this eventuality.

FIGURE 11.11   LANDING AT ILLAGA   Photo: Mal Creasey

All group members should be made aware of its existence and where to find it.

11.12   Civil unrest

Civil unrest and riots can happen anywhere. They are most common in places that are experiencing palpable tension or upheaval, where the smallest spark can ignite a situation that can make travel difficult or even impossible. If conflict erupts within a country or between countries, border crossings are often closed with immediate effect, potentially jeopardising any plans and often requiring a considerable change to the itinerary in order to vacate the situation. Before travelling abroad part of the research should involve reading news stories and studying the political situation of the area. It is also important to check for travel advice issued by the Foreign and Commonwealth Office. If there is a strong possibility of civil unrest, consider postponing or changing any plans. If you have to travel to a country or region where there could be potential problems check with your insurance company

first as some policies will not cover for civil unrest or similar situations. In certain circumstances the policy may become invalid if you are knowingly travelling to a country against the advice of an organisation such as the FCO.

Should civil instability erupt while you are travelling abroad, you may need to be evacuated. Making plans that cover for this eventuality may sound extreme and a little unnecessary, but much of the information gained from this process is useful for other aspects of trip planning.

- Know the locations of police stations, hospitals, embassies, airports and ports in the area.
- Carry the relevant phone numbers of embassies and consulates so that you can contact them while in-country.
- Carry the FCO contact details and consider registering online for the 'LOCATE' service *(see earlier in this chapter on page 152)*.
- If travelling abroad in an unstable country, call the relevant embassy to register and let them know of your presence.
- Keep an emergency credit card, a small supply of cash and some travellers cheques with your passport. During civil unrest, money can some-

times buy you out of awkward situations and will usually be essential to facilitate any evacuation.

While in-country try to pay attention to what's going on around you, especially when in towns or cities and large groups of people. In the weeks, days or hours preceding any unrest, residents of an area can often tell that something is about to happen. If local people, police, or consulate staff warn of the possibility of impending action, leave the area as quickly as is safely possible.

If caught up in a situation try to avoid large groups of people, especially demonstrations. The more people gathered together in one place, the greater the chance of a riot. Stay away from demonstrations as even peaceful protests can quickly turn violent and, if the atmosphere is already tense, consider avoiding festivals or other events where people crowd together.

Avoid public transportation, especially bus and train stations. These places may become hopelessly and dangerously overcrowded. Even airports can become swamped, so it's best to call in advance or check the situation with the embassy. If using an in-country agent seek their advice and support.

Appendices

TAGHIA, MOROCCO

Photo: Steve Long

A.1 Resources

Useful websites and further reading:

A1.1 Planning and preparation

Books

Winser S. (2004) *Royal Geographical Society Expedition Handbook* Profile Books
Various *Rough Guides*
Various *Lonely Planet Publications*
Deegan P. (2002) *Mountain Travellers Handbook* BMC

Websites

The British Mountaineering Council
www.thebmc.co.uk
The Royal Geographical Society
www.rgs.org
Foreign and Commonwealth Office (FCO)
www.fco.gov.uk/travel
Adventure M-apps
www.adventurem-apps.com

A1.2 Environment

Websites

Leave No Trace
www.lnt.org
International Porter Protection Group
www.ippg.net
International Mountaineering and Climbing Federation UIAA
www.theuiaa.org
UNEP World Conservation Monitoring Centre
www.unep-wcmc.org

A1.3 Staying healthy

Books

Birch K., MacLaren D. and George K. (2004) *Sport and Exercise Physiology* Taylor & Francis
Armstrong L.E. (1999) *Performing in Extreme Environments* Human Kinetics Publishers
Johnson C., Anderson S., Dallimore J. and Winser S. (2008) *Oxford Handbook of Expedition and Wilderness Medicine* OUP Oxford
Warrell D. and Anderson S. (2002) *Expedition Medicine (Royal Geographical Society)* Profile Books
Duff J. and Gormly P. (2007) *Pocket First Aid and Wilderness Medicine (Mini Guides)* Cicerone Press

Websites

World Health Organization
www.who.int
Hospital for Tropical Diseases
www.thehtd.org
Medical Advisory Service for Travellers Abroad
www.masta-travel-health.com
Fit for travel (Scottish NHS)
www.fitfortravel.scot.nhs.uk

A1.4 Trekking at altitude

Books

Pollard A. J. and Murdoch D. R. (2003)
The High Altitude Medicine Handbook
Radcliffe Publishing Ltd
Bezruchka S. (2005) *Altitude Illness: Prevention
& Treatment* Mountaineers Books

Websites

Medical expeditions
www.medex.org.uk
Expedition and Wilderness Medicine
www.expeditionmedicine.co.uk

A1.5 Navigation

Books

Forte C. (2012) *Navigation in the Mountains*
MTUK Publications
Cliff P. (1991) *Mountain Navigation*
Menasha Ridge Press Inc.
Letham L. (2001) *GPS Made Easy*
Mountaineers Books

Websites

Magnetic declination information
www.magnetic-declination.com
The Map Shop
www.themapshop.co.uk
Stanfords (international maps and guides)
www.stanfords.co.uk
Garmin (GPS information)
www.garmin.com
Satmap (GPS and Digital mapping)
www.satmap.com
Memory Map (Digital mapping)
www.memory-map.co.uk

A1.6 Weather

Books

Barry R. and Chorley R. (2003) *Atmosphere,
Weather and Climate* Routledge
Dunlop S. (2004) *Weather (Collins Gem)*
Thomas M. (1997) *Weather for Climbers and
Hillwalkers* The History Press Ltd

Websites

Met Office
www.metoffice.gov.uk
BBC Weather Centre
www.bbc.co.uk/weather

A1.7 Snow

Books

Cunningham A. and Fyffe A. (2007)
Winter Skills MTUK Publications
McClung D. and Schaerer P. (2010) *Avalanche
Handbook* Mountaineers Books
Bolognesi R. (2007) *Avalanche!* Cicerone Press

Websites

National Snow & Ice Data Center
www.nsidc.org
*Sports Scotland Avalanche
Information Service*
www.sais.gov.uk

A1.8 Other useful sites

British Embassies Abroad
www.fco.gov.uk
UK Passport Office
**www.homeoffice.gov.uk/agencies-public-
bodies/ips/**
Cordee (guidebooks and maps)
www.cordee.co.uk

A.2 Kit Lists

A2.1 Medical kit

For expeditions adapted from *High Altitude Medicine handbook*

Altitude
- Diamox – Acetazolomide
- Nifedipine
- Dexamethasone

Analgesia
- Aspirin
- Paracetamol
- Stronger analgesics – Codeine phosphate, Diclofenic

Asthma and anaphylaxis
- EpiPen
- Sulbutamol inhaler – Ventolin

Ear and nose
- Hayfever spray
- Nasal decongestant

Eyes
- Eye wash

Gastrointestinal
- Diorylate – oral rehydration
- Lomotil
- Senna

Infections
- A broad spectrum antibiotic to deal with a wide range of infections
- An alternative antibiotic without penicillin

Malaria
- Antimalarials
- Mosquito repellent and net

Metabolic
- Glucagon
- Glucose gel

Sterilisation and cleaning
- Alcohol swabs
- Iodine
- Dettol soap

Skin
- Calamine lotion
- High factor sun block
- Acyclovir
- Hydrocortisone cream
- KY jelly
- White soft paraffin

Teeth
- Clove oil
- Cavit

Throat/Oral
- Bonjela
- Throat lozenges

FIGURE A2.01   ORGANISING EXPEDITION KIT
Photo: Iain Peter

FIGURE A2.02   TYPICAL BUSH PATH IN JAPAN

Photo: Steve Long

A2.2 Clothing and equipment

Choosing suitable clothing and equipment for a trek can be a bewildering experience. There are many guide books and text books that offer advice, so the focus of this section is to identify the requirements associated with trekking in both summer and winter conditions, remote and non-remote environments. The main consideration is often to reduce weight within the constraints of a budget.

A2.3 What to wear

While trekking a range of temperatures are likely to be encountered, either because of exter-nal conditions or varying energy requirements. The simple solution is to use layers of clothing that can be added or removed in order to cope with the weather *(see Figure A2.02).*

Base layer

The base layer (the layer of clothes next to the skin) should ideally be made out of synthetic material to allow perspiration to wick away from the skin. Cotton soaks up moisture and retains water next to the skin, cooling the body as it evaporates and should therefore be avoided.

Consider a long sleeve top to reduce the area of skin exposed to sunlight.

Mid layer

The range of fleece garments is huge. The main consideration is warmth verses bulkiness. Several thin micro-pile fleeces may be more beneficial in a range of weather conditions and temperatures than one big bulky fleece. A simple windproof top with ventilation zips is invaluable in dry but windy conditions.

Outer layer

Breathable waterproof fabrics are now readily available from a range of manufacturers and have vastly improved the comfort level for the trekker. The transport of perspiration away from the skin to the outside of the garment enables the trekker to regulate their body temperature and not get soaked from the inside out. In summer alpine conditions, a thin *Gore-Tex*® jacket may be sufficient, but in winter or at high altitude a thicker one may provide extra warmth. For pure warmth-to-weight ratio, a feather down jacket remains the best, particularly in the cold dry conditions found at altitude. Otherwise, in potential damp conditions, the synthetic duvet jacket or belay jacket is a very good option *(see Figure A2.03).*

FIGURE A2.03   TOUBKAL SUMMIT   Photo: Mike Rosser

Boots

Boots are probably the most important item of equipment for trekking and are essential for both safety and comfort. There is a huge range of type and construction of boots, many of which are designed and made for specific types of trekking. With this specialisation it is important to get boots that match the use to which they will be put and the conditions liable to be encountered. Any boot will, to some degree be a compromise – one which is good for kicking steps in snow may be less comfortable to walk long distances in. Since boots are such a vital piece of gear it is worth spending the time shopping around to get a pair to suit your needs. Go to a knowledgeable supplier, try on different makes and types and as boot design, manufacture and materials change every year, get as much advice as possible before making any choices. The option of hiring different boots for short periods to try out can be very worthwhile.

Suitable boots can usually be worn with one pair of good quality socks and be sufficiently warm but this is a matter of personal choice and circulation. Remember, too warm feet can mean wetting from sweating and ultimately colder toes. However, it is important that they are a good fit as wearing extra socks may well not be warmer if the boots are then too tight.

A2.4 Suggested kit lists

Items shown in italics are dependent on circumstances – summer or winter, remote or non-remote, camping or hut-to-hut expeditions.

Personal kit
* Rucksack *and liner*
* Emergency bivouac bag
* Waterproof jacket
* Waterproof trousers
* Map
* Compass
* *GPS*
* Head torch and spare batteries
* Walking boots
* *Sunglasses, sun hat and sun cream*
* *Goggles*
* Drink
* Lunch
* Water bottle
* Hat and gloves
* Spare warm layer
* Spare food
* Personal first aid and medication
* *Gaiters*
* Walking poles
* *Snowshoes*
* Camera

Group kit

- Group first aid
- *Medicine*
- *Blizzard bag*
- Group shelter
- Spare map and compass
- Spare warm layer
- *Mobile phone/sat phone or EPIRB*
- Repair kit
- Rope
- Sling and karabiners
- *Ice axe*
- *Water filter and purification methods*
- *Insect repellent*
- Spare food and warm drink
- Spare hat and gloves
- *Throw bag and floating rope*

Overnight – hut-based

- Sleeping bag liner
- Ear plugs
- *Dissolvable multi-vitamin tablets*
- Toiletries
- Small travel towel
- Spare clothes

Camping

- Sleeping mat
- Sleeping bag
- Tent
- Water container
- Stove and pans

- Fuel
- Large mug
- Bowl
- Spoon, knife, fork
- Duvet jacket, synthetic or down
- Spare clothing
- Barrels, kit bags, duffel bags

A2.5 Repair kit

Breaking an item of equipment while on a trek can make life difficult; in certain circumstances it could mean a radical change to your plans. A small repair kit containing a few useful items with which it is possible to make a temporary repair could save the day or even the trip.

- Small bag or container
- Small roll of duct tape
- Heavy duty cable ties
- Smaller cable ties
- Spare strap(s)
- Length of 4mm cord
- Multi-tool or pliers, screwdrivers and pocket knife
- Some specific spares depending on the nature of the activity
- Spares for snowshoes
- Spare ski pole strap and basket

A.3 Mountain Training Awards

The Mountain Training Boards were established in the 1960s in the home nations of England, Scotland, Wales and Northern Ireland to set appropriate standards and awards for leaders and to administer and develop the awards.

Mountain Training UK coordinates the work of the home nation training boards as well as administering specific awards.
www.mountain-training.org

What is involved in gaining a Mountain Training qualification?
Although the detail of each award varies there are a number of common elements to every scheme.

- **Registration:** Before attending any course candidates must be registered with the appropriate scheme.
- **Training Courses:** All the awards involve practical training delivered by specially approved training staff. The relevant awarding body monitors the standards of training. Some schemes have the facility to recognise relevant prior experience and training by granting exemptions from training.
- **Consolidation Period:** Training courses alone cannot turn people into effective leaders and for this reason it can take some time to consolidate the ideas put forward at training.
- **Assessment:** All the awards have mandatory practical assessments conducted by specially approved assessors. On successful completion of the assessment candidates are recognised as holding the relevant qualification.
- **Continuing Personal and Professional Development:** Having gained an award candidates are expected to maintain and record their involvement in the activities as both an individual and as a leader. Opportunities for further training are available through the Mountain Training Association or other specialist associations. **www.mountain-training.org**

A3.1 International Mountain Leader Award – IML

This scheme trains and assesses people in the skills required to be competent to take trekking parties to all mountain areas except on glaciers and where the techniques or equipment of alpinism are required. The international mountain leader can also operate on easy snow-covered terrain, providing it is of a gentle, nordic type in the middle mountains. The award is administered by Mountain Training UK and is valid throughout the European Community and recognised internationally.

Prior to registration candidates must hold the Mountain Leader Award and have logged twenty summer international quality mountain days and twenty winter quality days (UK or overseas). Candidates attend five days of training, which includes a half-day speed navigation test, and four days of assessment in summer conditions. They also attend IML winter training and assessment.

A3.2 Mountain Leader Award – ML

The mountains of the UK are remote, technical and exposed to harsh and unpredictable weather. This makes them a potentially hazardous place for a group of novice mountain walkers unless they have the benefit of supervision by a well trained and experienced leader. The Mountain Leader Scheme trains and assesses people in the skills required for the leadership of hill walking parties in summer conditions. The award is administered by the combined Mountain Training Boards and is valid throughout the United Kingdom and Ireland.

A3.3 Walking Group Leader Award – WGL

This award is for leaders of walking groups in non-mountainous hilly terrain, known variously as upland, moor, bog, hill, fell or down. Such areas can be subject to extreme weather conditions and require an element of self-sufficiency. The scheme seeks to develop the skills necessary to lead walking groups in these areas. The award is administered by the combined Mountain Training Boards and is valid throughout the United Kingdom and Ireland.

A3.4 Winter Mountain Leader Award – ML(W)

This scheme trains and assesses people in the skills required for the leadership of hill walking parties in winter conditions. The award is administered by Mountain Training Scotland and is valid throughout the United Kingdom and Ireland.

A3.5 Mountaineering Instructor Award – MIA

This scheme trains and assesses people in the skills required for instruction of mountaineering, including all aspects of rock climbing. The award is administered by Mountain Training UK and is valid throughout the United Kingdom and Ireland.

A3.6 Mountaineering Instructor Certificate – MIC

This scheme trains and assesses people in the skills required for instruction of mountaineering, both summer and winter, including snow, ice and rock climbing. The award is administered by Mountain Training UK and is valid throughout the United Kingdom and Ireland.

A3.7 IFMGA Mountain Guide

This scheme trains and assesses experienced people in the skills required for the provision of instruction and guiding services in climbing, skiing and mountaineering on rock, ice and snow in all conditions and all seasons at BMG and IFMGA international standards. The award is administered by the British Association of Mountain Guides and is valid world-wide.
www.bmg.org.uk

A.4 Mountaineering Councils

Association of British Climbing Walls
www.abcclimbingwalls.co.uk

British Mountaineering Council
BMC, 177–179 Burton Road,
Manchester M20 2BB
Tel: 0870 – 010 4878
Fax: 0161 – 445 4500
E-mail: office@thebmc.co.uk
www.thebmc.co.uk

Mountaineering Ireland
Sport HQ, 13 Joyce Way, Park West Business
Park, Dublin 12, Ireland
Tel: 00 3531 – 625 1115
Fax: 00 3531 – 625 1116
E-mail: info@mountaineering.ie
www.mountaineering.ie

Mountaineering Council of Scotland
MC of S, The Old Granary, West Mill Street,
Perth PH1 5QP
Tel: 01738 – 638 227
Fax: 01738 – 442 095
E-mail: info@mcofs.org.uk
www.mcofs.org.uk

A.5 Contributors

Editor's Note – John Cousins

This book has been a fantastic collaborative effort and the biographies below give you an idea of the experience and abilities of the major contributors. Many others have also helped at various stages of the project and I'd like to thank them all. Within Mountain Training Steve Long was involved with the original development, Sue Doyle has managed the financing of the project and Pete Stacey, Brian Griffiths, Mary Matthews, Andy Boorman and Anne Newcombe have been amongst those contributing to the overall development of our book series. In developing the text we've had technical input from Dino Heald with the water hazards section, Caroline Hale with Snowshoeing and Kev Sidford with Planning. Libby Peter helped match photos to text and Ros Morley did her customary excellent job of tidying up all of our spelling and grammar. Many thanks go to Bob Kinnaird, Pete Stacey, Steve Long, Rob Johnson and Mo Laurie for their photos. Jane Beagley, Simon Norris and Jon Barton at Vertebrate Graphics have done a fantastic job putting the book together while Richard Robinson and the staff at Cordee have advised us on marketing and distribution.

Writing Team

Carlo Forte

Carlo Forte is an International Mountain Leader and Chief Instructor at Plas y Brenin. He has trekked and climbed throughout Europe and also Greenland, Malaysia, Borneo, Nepal and Patagonia. Carlo has coordinated the contributions from all the chapter authors, wrote the *Navigation* and *Weather* sections and supplied many of the illustrations for his chapters.

Martin Chester

Martin Chester is an IFMGA Guide and Director of Training at Plas y Brenin. He has climbed and trekked throughout the Alps, the Andes and the Himalayas. He wrote the *Snow – A seasonal Approach* and *Snowshoeing* chapters as well as supplying many of these chapters' illustrations.

Helen Barnard

Helen Barnard is an International Mountain Leader and Senior Instructor at Plas y Brenin. She has trekked and climbed in Europe, Chile, Argentina, Canada, Tanzania and Australia. She has written the *Staying Healthy* and *Trekking at Altitude* chapters and supplied several illustrations to this book.

Contributors continued overleaf

Simon Hale

Simon Hale is an International Mountain Leader, IFMGA Guide and a Senior Instructor at Plas y Brenin. He has trekked, climbed and lead groups throughout the Alps, Mexico, Canada and America. Simon wrote the *Mountain Hazards* chapter and supplied many of the illustrations for this section.

Mike Raine

Mike Raine is an International Mountain Leader, former Geography teacher and Senior Instructor at Plas y Brenin. He has trekked and climbed throughout Europe and America. Mike wrote much of the original environment chapter for this book.

Mike Rosser

Mike Rosser is an International Mountain Leader, Operations Manager for Outlook Expeditions and lectures on Plas y Brenin's IML training courses on behalf of the Expedition Adviser's Panel. His first expedition as a student teacher was to Iceland in 1974 and since then he's climbed in over forty countries exploring new areas and making many first ascents. Mike wrote the planning chapter and contributed several photos to the book.

Dr. Dave Hillebrandt

Dr David Hillebrandt delivers units of the Diploma in Mountain Medicine at Plas y Brenin. He is an active mountaineer who combines his professional expertise with a passion for climbing in remote locations and he advises climbers and trekkers about the effects of altitude on known medical conditions. He provided technical editing support to the *Staying Healthy* and *Trekking at Altitude* chapters.

Keith Ball

Keith Ball is an International Mountain Leader and Mountaineering Instructor at Plas y Brenin. He has trekked and climbed extensively throughout Europe, also Greenland, Alaska, Nepal, Australia and Canada. He read through all the early drafts and provided internal technical editing for much of the text.

Louise Turner

Louise Turner is an International Mountain Leader, IFMGA Guide, a former Chief Instructor at Plas y Brenin and now works for Aiglon Colleg in Switzerland. She has trekked and climbed around the world and has made first ascents of vertical walls in Baffin, Borneo, Britain, Greenland, Jordan, Madagascar, Mali, Norway, Pakistan, Patagonia and Venezuela. Louise wrote the *'Dealing with Problems'* chapter.

Editing and production team

John Cousins
John Cousins is an IFMGA Guide and Executive Officer of Mountain Training UK. He has trekked and climbed around the world for over thirty years from New Zealand to Alaska and Malaysia to Kyrgyzstan. John is editor in chief and publisher for this book as well as providing a number of photos.

Iain Peter
Iain Peter is an IFMGA Guide and Consultant. He has trekked and climbed all over the world. Iain is the chair of MTUK's publications group and has overseen this book as well as providing technical editing support and a substantial number of photos.

Mal Creasey
Mal Creasey is an IFMGA Guide and Technical Officer of Mountain Training England. He has had over thirty Scottish Winter and Alpine seasons as well as numerous trips to far flung corners of the world. He has provided technical editing support and numerous photos to this book.

Jon Garside
Jon Garside is an International Mountain Leader and Training Officer of the British Mountaineering Council and Mountain Training England. He has trekked and climbed in Nepal, Kyrgyzstan, Bolivia, Peru, Norway, New Zealand, Tanzania and North America. Jon has provided technical editing support and several photos to this book.

Issie Inglis
Issie Inglis is an International Mountain Leader, current President of the British Association of International Mountain Leaders Creating and Managing Director of Adventure M-apps. She has climbed and trekked all over the world and lead trekking groups in the greater ranges of Nepal, India and Bhutan. She has provided technical editing for the text.

Will Manners
Will Manners is an International Mountain Leader and Technical Director for Outlook Expeditions. He has trekked and climbed in South Georgia, North and South America, Nepal, Africa and in Europe. Will has provided technical editing support and several photos to the book.

Nigel Williams
Nigel Williams is an International Mountain Leader and Director of Training at Glenmore Lodge. He has participated in more than 20 expeditions ranging from the Himalayan countries to Greenland, South Georgia and Alaska. Nigel has provided technical editing support and several of the photos for the book.

A.6 Index

W

Notes

Notes